EMPATH'S SURVIVAL GUIDE

How to Develop Your Gift, Set Boundaries, and Control Your Emotions (Emotional Intelligence, Empath, and Empath Workbook)

Alison L. Alverson

Also by Alison L. Alverson

Chakra Series Book 1
Chakra Healing For Beginners: The Complete Guide to Awaken and Balance Chakras for Self-Healing and Positive Energy

Chakra Series Book 2
Chakra Healing For Beginners: Discover 35 Self-Healing Techniques to Awaken and Balance Chakras for Health and Positive Energy

Empath Series Book 1
Empath: An Extensive Guide for Developing Your Gift of Intuition to Thrive in Life

Empath Series Book 2
Empath Workbook: Discover 50 Successful Tips To Boost your Emotional, Physical And Spiritual Energy

Standalone

Emotional Intelligence : 21 Effective Tips To Boost Your EQ (A Practical Guide To Mastering Emotions, Improving Social Skills & Fulfilling Relationships For A Happy And Successful Life)
Empath's Survival Guide: How to Develop Your gift, Set Boundaries, and Control Your Emotions (Emotional Intelligence, Empath, and Empath Workbook)

Watch for more at www.alisonalverson.com.

Table of Contents

EMOTIONAL INTELLIGENCE

21 Effective Tips To Boost Your EQ

A Practical Guide To Mastering Emotions, Improving Social Skills & Fulfilling Relationships For A Happy And Successful Life

Alison L. Alverson

Introduction

"You will continue to suffer if you have an emotional reaction to everything that is said to you. The power is sitting back and observing things with logic. True power is restraint. If words control you that means everyone else can control you. Breathe and allow things to pass"

Warren Buffett

"*Yes, this is true.*" That was my answer when I first laid my eyes on those thunderous words. It was a message that saved me when I needed it. Let me tell you my story. I was smart enough to graduate with high grades in college. I always had a concept that if you want to live a good life, you must be intelligent. I found a new job and was preparing myself for the interview. I was ready for this job and I was 90% sure I was going to get the job.

The next day when I went for the interview, everything was upside down. I couldn't control my anxiety, so I did badly. The result was that I lost that incredible job. I was frustrated and was asking myself these questions; "**Why did I screw things up?**", '**How could my emotions overcome my intelligence?**" The next day I decided to be optimistic and move on. After that, I got a call from my friend who invited me to her party. I accepted it because I wanted to have some fun.

During the party, I saw one of my old friends and I waved at her, but she didn't wave back. I felt ignored. But I said to myself I would not let this upset me. The party was cool, and I was happy to be there. When I was ready to leave, I met that same girl who ignored me (as I thought). She smiled at me and asked me where I had been because she didn't see me. She was nice and I had misunderstood her. I left the party. While I was driving my car, a man crossed the street talking on his phone. I pressed the brakes of the car at the last moment. I was furious. I shouted and abused him. When I got home, I was in a bad mood. My pleasant day blew up in a second. I sat down silent for a while and looked to myself in the mirror. Then I start talking to myself," **What is going on?" "Why are my emotions upside down?" "I hate losing my temper"**

In the morning, I was happy. In the afternoon, I was optimistic. At night, I was frustrated.... etc. "**How could anyone make me angry that easily? How could a person or a thing have the power to change my mood in a moment?"** I felt like my life was controlled by emotions. Then I heard an alarm on my phone. It was a post on one of my Facebook groups. When I opened it, it was Warren's quote. I was shocked as if the universe had heard me and sent the solution to my questions by saying "**Hey dude, wake up and control your emotions if you want to live happily before it is too late.**"

From here, I started searching for things like "What are emotions? How can I handle it?" and "Which one is more important intelligence or emotions?" This led me to learn about the term "**Emotional Intelligence**" and read a lot about it because I intended to reach my own peace of mind. I admit it was a little bit difficult to control my feelings at the beginning. I tried different strategies, but I failed. I had ups and downs. I tried others and went through challenges until I found the effective steps which would enhance my emotional intelligence and which also led me here.

Once I discovered what emotional intelligence was all about and how to have it, I thought that it was time to share those thoughts with the world. After all, there must be others like me, who are searching for answers and who are unable to find them. This book is based upon my vast experience of taking control of my life. Believe me, emotional intelligence is a huge part of that. You may think that money can buy you the kind of happiness you believe is what everyone seeks. However,

I am here to tell you that without emotional intelligence, that money won't even touch the sides.

This is my journey, but it's worded in such a way that it can be the reader's journey too as the steps toward emotional intelligence can be taken by anyone who has the will to move forward in their lives and wants to see life from a different and new perspective. I did and you can too. However, you do need to understand the process and my research and my own experience can help you. I didn't have that help and when the light dawned on me and I discovered the secret to this kind of inner happiness, I was bursting with joy to share it with others who may, like me, have found themselves lost in the maze of life. If this is you, the book can change your whole way of life as it did mine. That is my hope, that as you keep reading the book, you find your own sense of wellbeing and happiness, and are able to experience the joy that comes with that acceptance of self.

I highly encourage you to join our friendly community Facebook to maximize the value you receive from this book. What often helps a lot is connecting with other like-minded people whom you can relate to, get support, and learn from on how to navigate Life's challenges. This can be an excellent support network for you.

It would be great to connect with you there,

To Join Our Friendly Support Group visit: http://bit.ly/2pg5AEE

What are Emotions and How They Influence Our Thinking?

Emotions are feelings that come into your mind and that affect how you react to given stimuli. You feel joy when you think of certain things, or you feel disgust at things that fall outside the scope of the acceptable. These are normal reactions that your brain uses to balance your reactions to the things that happen around you. Thus, sadness and all of the emotions you feel are affected by outside influence. They can also be triggered by your reactions to outside influence, so you can't blame the world entirely for the way that you feel. You can, however, blame your reaction to those circumstances and that's something that you have control over. You may not know it yet, but we all do, and emotional intelligence is what makes the difference. Those who do not have emotional intelligence may find themselves experiencing the negativity of emotions such as:

- Anger
- Frustration
- Jealousy
- Rage

But these are not the only negative emotions. Negative emotions are those, which cause a negative reaction within your mind. You may say that you have no control over these, but when you adopt an emotionally intelligent stance, you will find that you have more control than you give yourself credit for because your approach is different. Let's look at the seven basic emotions:

- **Anger**
- **Happiness**
- **Sadness**
- **Fear**
- **Surprise**
- **Contempt**
- **Disgust**

If you look at that list, you will see that more of them are negative than positive and it may surprise you to find that the mind thinks negative thoughts more than it thinks positive ones. So what's going on in the mind when it becomes emotional? Well, you would have to look for scientific proof of what's going on, but to you, you feel overwhelmed by the negativity or can even feel euphoric when you experience the joy of happiness. Why would these different emotions have such a profound effect on the way that you relate to your life? These were all questions that I had about emotions when I was taking the same journey as you are and my findings were rather enlightening.

According to neuroscientist Antonio Damasio, the feelings that we get as humans derive from external influences and he has done much work to try and determine what happens when an emotion is evoked. Damasio explains that we associate feelings with emotions and assume that certain things will happen following experiencing something that evokes a certain emotion. What's actually happening inside the brain is that certain reactions to a stimuli are triggered because the body is going into a response to what we have seen. Thus, it's common that we feel our heartbeat increasing when we are stressed. We may find that blood pressure rises or that we have sweaty palms. That's when we experience feelings such as pain.

So how do we gain better control of the way that external influences make the body react? You have to turn to science to find the answers to that. PET scanning and MRI studies show that different areas of the brain are affected by different emotions and that means that once we know the reactions, we can alter our emotions to help ourselves to remain calm and subjective, rather than simply going with the emotion being felt. Let's take a look at the way the emotion of happiness sparks off activity in different areas of the brain.

Happiness – This affects the right frontal cortex. There are also feelings within the amygdala or center for feelings and the awareness part of the brain in the frontal cortex.

There are a whole load of references which show you the different areas of the brain affected by emotions, but more interesting than that is the work that is being done by the scientific world and the Dalai Lama based upon MRI scans that were done on Buddhist monks. These experiments were done at the New York University and showed that monks were able to control the see-sawing effect of the brain jumping from one emotion to the next or from outside influence to internal influence. Dr. Josipovic, Research Assistant and Adjunct Professor at the New York University stated:

"Meditation research, particularly in the last 10 years or so, has shown to be very promising because it points to an ability of the brain to change and optimize in a way we didn't know previously was possible."

If you need further proof of this , then watching a video by a neuroscientist may awaken you to the truth about the way that the brain reacts to the world around you and backs up the claims that people who experience compassion and humility in their approach to life tend to find that their emotions are more balanced and easier to live with. Dr. Sarah Lazar makes interesting points based on her experience as a neurosurgeon and upon her own trial at controlling emotions with the use of meditation. In her case, the results were quite amazing, particularly since she was not expecting the results that she got. She found that meditational practice could actually change the shape of part of the brain and that this change brought about peaceful thoughts and the ability to be more compassionate and capable of using emotions to positive effect.

The process of thinking in an emotional way and what it does to the brain

You may think that emotions are just thoughts, but they trigger off certain actions in the brain. For example, an MIT study revealed how there are two areas in the brain that process emotions – these are located within the amygdala area of the brain. Knowing this, experiments were done on mice to watch the activity within the brain during instances when the mice were offered pleasurable reward in the way of sugar cubes. It was certainly proven that negative effects and positive effects caused different reactions in the brain and that the amygdala area of the brain connects to different regions, which are triggered into action by the thought of reward or by negativity. What the scientists said after this experiment was:

“We are exploring the interactions between these different projections, and we think that could be a key to how we so quickly select an appropriate action when we’re presented with a stimulus,”

This is also backed up by the idea that the habits that we adopt will also affect the emotional response of the human being to different stimuli. Thus, for one person a very positive stimuli could prove negative to someone else. Therefore, you have to know your own habits and the emotions that are triggered by certain actions within your life before you can control those reactions. Look at the sense of reward, for example. If an emotion leads you to some kind of reward, then you feel good about it. However, if it doesn’t, it can lead to negative thoughts and negative consequences. It is important therefore that you note down the feelings or emotions that you experience during the course of a day and watch for differences in your comportment or attitude as these will have been events that are triggered within the amygdala region. In the case of the meditators, these were people who were able to balance the effects and therefore did not feel extreme emotions and were able to feel the bliss of happiness.

How emotions influence our thinking

If you experience a negative emotion, you are likely to analyze it and thus make it larger than it originally was. People who are depressed tend to over analyze and are unable to see any reward at the end of their thinking. However, people who are well balanced and whose lives are considered to be within “norms” can still over-react to a stimuli. As I said in the opening, I got mad at the man crossing the street. In my case, the shock of what was happening that was beyond my control triggered anger, but if you allow outside influences to do that to you, then you are not fully in control of the life that you are living. In fact, you are doing exactly what Warren Buffett suggests and letting people control your life and your response to life. It’s like letting go of responsibility and making everyone around you to blame for the way that you feel. In fact, you are the person in the driving seat if you wish to be, and that's the purpose of this book, to bring you to a place where you actually are.

If you have self-esteem problems, these also come from an outside influence in many cases. For example, how many times have people told you that you are inadequate in some way? Your parents may have derided you for your choices. Your friends may not like your sense of style. You may be overweight and measure yourself against society norms, but the point of it all is that it's the way that you see it that matters and if you can adjust your own view of self, you can get over the fact that emotions are now in turmoil and take back control of your own life. The first fact to face is that whatever emotions are doing to you, as an individual, your thoughts and actions are being influenced by them. Thus, the less you expose yourself to negative influences or allow them to become negative, the more likely you are to feel in control of your emotions. It is a case of being in control of the way that you react to any given stimuli. Yes, of course, you will be sad sometimes, but that doesn't have to affect your thought processes if you know how to handle sadness. The best thing about emotional intelligence is that you get to drive the car and that's when life gets really interesting.

Emotions can trigger a spiral of negative thoughts or euphoria to the extreme. However, when you know more about how it all works and are able to harness this power, you find that you are more receptive to the emotions being felt by others and that you are totally in control of your own emotions and they do not trigger so much negativity that you become out of control. Your inner strength will ensure that even when you are met by negative emotions, you will have the ability to cope with them in an emotionally intelligent manner. Think about the last time that you encountered a negative emotion. Someone said something that made you angry. The situation is that you can either judge this as being a passing event or you can do what most people do and blow it up into a huge problem that is larger than life. Most people do the latter, just like I did when someone crossed the road in front of me. By the time you have finished reading this book, you will know how to better deal with the thought processes that follow your emotions, but you will also know how to control those emotions in the first place, by introducing a different set of standards – those that do not judge.

The Concept of Emotional Intelligence

We are all aware of people measuring their IQ. This is supposed to measure the intelligence of individuals, but more and more employers are now seeing that without the added content to a character of emotional intelligence, these IQ numbers are relatively meaningless. A good test of both gives a much more balanced picture of who someone is. So who came up with the idea of emotional intelligence? Well, to go back to its roots, you need to look back to the 1990s. That isn't that long ago, but Peter Salovey and John D. Mayer published an article is March 1990, that explains the importance of being able to evaluate emotions in both ourselves and others, in order to have emotional intelligence. So what's different about the skills that emotionally intelligent people have and those that don't? keep reading to find out.

It has been suggested for years that emotions rule our motivation to do things. If we feel positive, for example, we have more control over our motivation and are more likely to succeed. However, it goes much deeper than this simple analogy. As the number of people who are stressed increases, one has to question whether their lack of motivation comes from the overwhelming negativity of emotions that subjects feel they have no control over. Salovey and Mayer started their paper by introducing ideas that people accept, i.e., that emotions are our responses to different stimuli which can be put together and represent:

- *Our physiological responses*
- *Our cognitive responses*
- *Our motivational responses*
- *Our experiential responses*

If we know that, then we have to work out what it means to be emotionally intelligent against what it means to have a high IQ. One does not rely upon the other and the paper written by Salovey and Mayer clearly shows this. Thus, someone with a high IQ may not be particularly emotionally intelligent and vice versa. Neither depends on each other. They are separate responses to events that happen in the course of a lifetime. One uses logic to solve problems and the other uses emotional responses to solve problems. You could also relate your thoughts to social intelligence and people who experience this, for example, would be people who are good at managing others. However, social intelligence has also been linked to manipulation and is not, therefore, a good measure against emotional intelligence, which is not only aware of the moves of others, but also of self within that set situation. Emotionally intelligent people are able to perceive things that are not tangible. They are able to perceive other people's emotions accurately and also handle their own emotions in a suitable manner so that everyone gains some form of positivity from this encounter.

There was a rather good diagram in the paper by Salovey and Mayer, which shows the uses to which emotional intelligence can be put. It goes something like this. You start with emotional intelligence and you have a choice of how you use that intelligence. The tree that formed the diagram explains that the levels of emotional intelligence are varied. For example, you may use it for any one of the following:

- Being able to appraise and express emotions
- Being able to regulate emotions in ourselves and others
- Using emotion for the following:

  - *Creative thinking*
  - *Flexible planning*
  - *Redirecting attention where needed*
  - *Or finding motivation*

You can see by this list that this gives an emotionally intelligent person a lot of leverage. Placed in an emotional situation, they will be able to understand their own emotions and be empathetic toward the emotions of someone else. Let's face it, the guy who walked in front of my car that night got as big a shock as I did, but at that time, I was only seeing the picture from a very limited place in my mind. Had I exercised emotional intelligence at that time, I would have been able to use flexibility and redirect my attention to my own situation without having experienced anger.

Something very interesting about the paper on emotions was that it demonstrated that one needed to have a good understanding of emotions in order to handle them and that this extraordinary ability to handle emotions comes from empathy and experiential events. The paper questioned why we need negative emotions, but in reality, unless we experience them and know what they are and what they feel like, how do we derive joy when life shows us the other extreme. A good knowledge of both is necessary in order to be emotionally intelligent.

Presence of mind is another expression that has been used to explain the difference between someone who has emotional intelligence and someone who has not. For example, would you turn up for an interview looking inappropriate? Would you have an idea of the kind of questions you are likely to be asked and by whom? Those who prepare themselves for events that happen in their lives are usually fairly emotionally intelligent, but it goes further than simple preparation. An emotionally intelligent person will know how to impress the interviewers. They are also able to uplift others who may be in a sadder place than they are. They are not afraid of approaching sadness with an empathetic eye and much of their behavior is geared toward making a situation better, rather than looking at it in a negative manner. Emotionally intelligent people are also able to learn from bad situations and use this information to teach them different approaches, which help to swing the balance in favor of the positive. Their flexible approach works and faced with colleagues who are difficult and diverse, an emotionally intelligent person comes up with creative solutions that allow each of those diverse and difficult people to excel in the area of the task at hand that they know will motivate them.

Emotionally intelligent people opt for growth rather than pleasure and can derive pleasure from growth, rather than buying into a commercialized world where people believe that you can buy solutions to your problems.

The way that your emotions affect your thought processes is simple. If you get out of bed in the morning with a negative viewpoint and negative emotions, you are likely to have a worse day than someone who starts the day with optimism and enthusiasm. Emotions that are negative erode the thought processes. They encourage the wrong kind of responses, which is why the number of people suffering from stress in this day and age is increasing. There have been several studies into the effect of emotions and it is worthwhile reading from the links at the end of the book and watching the video suggested earlier in this chapter.

Charles Darwin formed the opinion that emotions were important to human beings and that they helped them in their quest for survival. He was also smart enough to know that emotions are adaptable. Psychologists William James and Carl Lang were of the opinion that emotions didn't cause reactions, but that reactions caused emotions. Thus if you were being chased by a tiger and your heartbeat fast, it would be the physiological symptoms that caused the emotions to go into overdrive, rather than fear being the reason why you ran. Conversely, Richard Lazarus believed that the first feeling of initial fear triggered the fight or flight response within the body and that the emotion of fear came first. Both Darwin and James believed that emotions could be betrayed by the study of facial features and expressions, giving light to the origins of what we know today as body language.

Is EQ better than IQ?

Since EQ is now recognized as important in interviews and is being taken seriously by the working world, is it as important as IQ? Yes, I asked myself this several times during my adventures into discovering how to master my emotions. In fact, an intelligent person uses education to further his career. He has learned the basics and therefore we know that his brain is capable of picking up systems and techniques that are involved in the learning process. However, that doesn't mean that he was going to be good with people and it certainly doesn't imply that he will derive any happiness out of his learning. That's where emotional intelligence comes into play. An emotionally intelligent person will be aware of himself and of the people around him. He won't lose his temper or go off on a tangent when the unexpected happens. Instead, he will use his automatic responses creatively and will come up with creative solutions.

Let us examine the major differences between IQ and EQ

- *IQ is a measurement of a person's ability to acquire knowledge*

- *This ability is something that someone with a high IQ is born with*

- *The IQ measures the ability to deal with mental challenges, as far as this relates to learning new things.*

- *IQ is measured within set parameters*

EQ, on the other hand, is a measurement of someone's ability to accept self and accept others.

- *It is also the ability to work with the emotions of self and the emotions of others.*

- *It is able to come up with creative solutions, rather than standardized ones and is adaptable.*

- *EQ is a measurement that can be improved upon whereas IQ is not.*

You can see from the above that both have their virtues, but that emotional intelligence wins the draw because you are able to increase it by practicing new things and learning to understand the mentality of people around you. You are more likely to feel empathy and also to feel compassion, as well as having a better understanding of self. That's a huge subject that many intellects avoid, preferring to base all of their judgments onset models, rather than being adaptable enough to change views when circumstances call for it.

What scientific evidence exists that EQ is more important than IQ?

New Hampshire psychologists Mayer and Salovey, mentioned earlier in this book, believed that emotional intelligence made a vast difference between performing a task and performing it in an outstanding way. One of the examples used was the difference between building a bridge and creating a landscape by building a beautiful bridge. The engineering folk would argue that if the bridge works, then why does it need to be pleasant to the eye? However, those with emotional intelligence would argue that the bridge should inspire and should fit with the environment into which it is to be placed.

Later work by Goleman, based on the principle that IQ and EQ exist and that EQ is the interaction of the human being with himself and others, the MRI scans that were taken showed levels of activity differed between the brain activity during logical thinking and emotional thinking. We know that the amygdala and frontal lobes of the brain show higher activity when emotional tasks were performed. We also know from the scans done on Buddhist monks that the balance of the two separate parts of the amygdala was more defined and that people who have emotional intelligence tend to suffer less from the effects of stress because they have better control of their emotions and can interact easily with others.

The findings by scientists confirmed that people who are emotionally intelligent are likely to exhibit the following advantages:

- They are more aware of themselves and their behavior toward others

- They are able to manage their emotions and this gave them the ability to bounce back when things went wrong

- They needed little motivation because their positivity gave them the motivation that they needed to be productive

- They are able to handle the emotions of others and be empathetic toward them, as well as being able to be compassionate and more understanding of diverse emotional situations.

- They are able to handle people and use their emotional intelligence to get the best from them in the workplace.

These are all positive traits that come with being emotionally intelligent and my work took me further because I had a need inside me to improve the emotional responses that I made toward the world around me. Anger was perceived as an inappropriate response, although anger can sometimes be beneficial in that it may motivate one to improve or to get things right next time. The negative emotions need to be lessened but also recognized for what they are so that solutions can be found to problems as and when they arise. For example, instead of being angry with the man who crossed the road in front of my car, I would be more careful in my approach toward places where pedestrians were likely to cross. You have to adjust your thinking, rather than letting events take precedence over the way that your mind works.

Similarly, when I saw the girl at the party, as described in the earlier part of the book, I assumed that she was shunning me because I was unable to read her emotions and tune into them. When reading up on this kind of miscommunication, I was interested to know why emotional intelligence enhances your ability to read situations. In fact, it makes you dig deeper than the surface and had I done that in the party situation, I may have had a much more pleasant experience because I would not have let my emotional thoughts rule my negative state of mind and would have been more open and receptive to other people's feelings and body language.

So do employers now use EQ in their interview processes?

OfficeTeam did a survey and asked employers whether they measure EQ at interview stage and if so how they did it. The survey involved 600 human research managers and up to 800 employees and 99 percent said that it was used. For example, the kind of questions an employer would ask would be geared to knowing the EQ from the answers given. Typical questions would outline how an applicant felt about handling failure or mixing with other employees, as well as their emotional comportment in general. Thus, it should be taken relatively seriously in the professional field. The amount of blame placed on others also gives employers a good idea of the applicant's emotional intelligence as someone who is emotionally intelligent would rationalize their failures rather than playing the blame game.

The most important thing to remember which is the reason I wrote this book is that emotional intelligence can be improved with effort, whereas IQ is the same throughout your life. Thus, if you want to increase your chances at success, then emotional intelligence is the way to go. It changes your approach to life. It changes your reactions to other people, it helps you to know your own limitations and to work toward improving

any limitation that you feel you may currently have. It's indeed a very painful journey at first, but once you get accustomed to knowing who you are in relationship to the world around you, it increases your chances of success. It was a hard pill for me to swallow, but once I took that route, the changes in my life were amazing. That's why I wanted to get it all down on paper so that you too can experience increasing your EQ and thus increasing the likelihood of success in everything that you do in your life.

Why is EQ so important?

If you cannot manage your emotions and the emotions of others, your life is disadvantaged in many ways. In this chapter, I will look at those ways so that you get a better understanding of why it's important to increase your EQ level if you want to make the most of your life.

Work performance

You may have a very high IQ, but if you are not a people person, then you are not a great leader. You may have known bosses during the course of your life that will never really go far in their lives because they feel no empathy, have little patience for their staff and really don't know how to work as a team. They are also the people who will gladly take credit for the things that have been achieved by others. Anyone of these traits can follow a person if they have no EQ. They simply don't care about others enough to let them enter the equation. Now, let's look at how EQ changes work performance.

Teamwork

Someone with EQ will know the members of staff and will be aware of their emotional strengths and weaknesses. They will not place the wrong members of the team in positions of vulnerability. Instead, they will place team members where their strengths lie because they will get better results. For example, some people work better independently of others and they would be placed in jobs that allow them that freedom to work alone but within the level of the capability. Others like to be in a team and work well with team members. These are people a manager with a high EQ would place together so that they are able to bring out the best in each other.

Promotion

Over the years, employment has become more and more important. It doesn't matter if you have a glowing resume if you don't have EQ, it is likely that you will be passed over for promotion. The reason isn't your level of activity or even your capability. Where the weakness lies in that you tend to hoard your work, thinking you are the best person to do it. You tend to clear your desk regularly because you think you need to prove that you can go above and beyond what is normal. The problem with this theory is that you are not management material. You don't know how to share your workload or teach others. You don't encourage others to succeed. You don't know how to delegate and will fail as a manager because of all of these faults, even though you may be more qualified on paper and have a higher IQ. Emotional intelligence means that you are better placed for promotion. You know how to handle people and you face the workload with enthusiasm and positivity that drives others.

Your work performance is better because you know how to prioritize. You also know how to handle your time if you have emotional intelligence because you know your own weaknesses and work around them, rather than seeing them as flaws and hiding them. You are able to gauge people better and can enlist help from the right people, thus getting the job done more efficiently. Your success rate will also be high and even if you fail, you will use failures as learning curves rather than become frustrated by them.

When you look at top entrepreneurs like Virgin boss, Richard Branson, you will find that they don't purport to be perfect or to have perfect solutions. They employ good people to do the jobs they need to be done, and Richard has said that he embraces mistakes rather than regrets them because they teach him better ways to do things. That's what EQ does. He is empathetic with his employees and knows their strengths and weaknesses and works toward providing them with a workplace that is dynamic and that feeds their enthusiasm rather than dampening it.

Mental Health

This is a massive subject. Do you know the percentage of people being treated for stress related ailments in the US in one year? There are 43.8 billion human beings who are treated for some kind of mental illness in the United States every single year and the numbers are not going down. The statistics mentioned were gathered on a very reputable website that collates numbers relating to mental health called The National Alliance on Mental Health. I mentioned earlier in the book that scientists and psychologists have even been having meetings with the Dalai Lama in order to find out how systems in use by Buddhists can be used in the general population to help lower these numbers.

In this day and age, there is so much stress placed on the modern population that they are ill equipped to deal with it. Thus, more and more classes have been introduced in mindfulness and meditation to slow down that process of overthinking things and to be able to provide practitioners with the opportunity to get to know themselves and to feel that they fit into modern society in a more acceptable way. From self-love to gratitude, the feelings that human beings go through in their lives are as a direct result of emotional input. The negativity that you feel comes from emotions. The positivity that you experience also comes from emotions, but the brain is more likely to think in the negative form than the positive one. It's the survival instinct that every human being was born with. The problem with this is that it also makes us skeptical and with so many interferences from this technical age, human beings have forgotten to use things such as instinct or gut feeling because their lives don't give them the time to experience these and they are also influenced by the media and the expected reactions of society in general.

What interested me the most about this kind of solution is that it's there for everyone who chooses to pursue it. It is not exclusive like high IQ is. With training, anyone can experience emotional intelligence and profit from it. In the chapter that deals with solutions and steps to increase your emotional intelligence, you will find that some of these seem basic, but we have lost touch with basics these days and put all of our trust on modern technology to solve problems that are not machine made. These are emotional problems that come to the mind through negative thinking, which is also inherent with the human race. The National Science Foundation published a paper in 2005 and what this showed was that the thoughts that come to your mind take a pattern.

95 percent of your thoughts are repetitive thoughts. This means that they are thoughts that run through your mind during the course of your life and may even be day to day. For example, "I must make the dinner" or "I must switch off the alarm." Everything that forms the thoughts centered upon tasks that you do are repetitive thoughts. On top of that, they found that 80 percent of your thoughts are negative. These are the "What if..." or "I wish I had..." type of thoughts or the thoughts that critique yourself or others. That's a huge percentage isn't it? So how can you expect yourself to be in control of your mental welfare when the human brain is throwing this many negative thoughts into your life each day? The answer is to learn to harness those thoughts and that's what mindfulness and meditation teach you to do. You may have heard of people using things like affirmations or being asked to replace negative thoughts with positive responses and the reason that this is done is so that the subconscious mind registers the new reaction because it is repeated sufficient times to become a habit that replaces the negative approach.

Mindfulness has been used on mental health patients in the United Kingdom for some time now and is showing great success. If you watched the video that I directed you to earlier by the neuroscientist, you will also have had her confirmation that this simple change in your approach to life helps you to feel happier and more capable of being positive toward others. Mental health relies upon positive input and that doesn't have to be from others. If you rely too much on the approval of others, then you are not looking into your own way of life in an emotionally intelligent manner. You are using others for props and without their validation, you feel that you are not worthy. That's why people are encouraged to learn about themselves and learn to accept self rather than depending upon others for validation that may not happen.

Relationships

There's a lot of give and take with a successful relationship, but it's much more than that. When someone is comfortable in the skin they are in, they offer more to their friendships. They are not needy. They do not rely upon friends for positive input but can create this positive input within themselves. During the course of my life, I have known people who say they "cannot" cope alone. The thing is that everyone can if they have the emotional intelligence to do it. It starts with the thoughts that you have and the emotions with which they are greeted. If you do not have self-love, it's unreasonable to expect love from others. Why would they want someone who is incomplete? To compensate for this, many people use themselves as doormats because it makes them feel validated. She needs me to babysit whenever she wants to go out. He needs me because I have purposely not let him near the kitchen and if I wasn't there, he would starve. Come on, be real. If you are in a relationship that is worth its salt and you are also emotionally intelligent you realize that your life and the life of a partner or lover are two separate things. Each has their own level of personal growth. In an ideal situation with someone who is emotionally intelligent, they will encourage you to learn new things or to be that individual that you are, rather than restraining you in some way. That control that you let others have over who you are shows a decided lack of emotional intelligence, but as I said in a previous chapter, you don't have to stay stuck in that situation, because emotional intelligence can be learned.

Conflict resolution

People with a high level of emotional intelligence are able to adjust situations more easily because they don't look at failure in the same way as those who only have IQ and who may be phased by failure. They look at conflicts from many angles and are able to take all sides into account, rather than seeing the conflict from a myopic viewpoint.

Success and Leadership

Those with a good strong emotional intelligence make better leaders and experience more success because their success is not single-minded. They are able to work well with others and supervise in a better way than those with a high IQ. They are people friendly and that means that they will take into account the personal strengths and weaknesses of others, thus producing a better and quicker result. They lead by example, not by fear and those who work for them are impressed at their ability to adjust to the variety of situations that are presented in a world of constant competition.

These are the reasons why emotional intelligence is much more important than IQ. You determine the level of emotional intelligence by learning how to increase it and make your life so much more than it is now by doing just that.

12 Signs of Low Emotional Intelligence People

Low emotional intelligence means that people fly off the hand easily because they are not adaptable. It also means that much of the time they are not aware of their emotional entanglement in everyday situations. These are people who may lose their temper easily, and who play the blame game because they don't want to take responsibility for when things go wrong. If you deal with people with low emotional intelligence you are likely to experience the following.

Let's look at some questions that will help you to decide how emotionally intelligent people around you are and how it may affect you:

1. **Does your partner get frustrated and angry at life?** The chances are that he/she is more frustrated with herself or himself because they are not getting the same as you are from the relationship. Beware. It may take a great deal of patience on your part to put things right, including trying to bolster your partner's understanding of emotional intelligence.

1. **Does your boss shout a lot?** – You may find that you are scared of your boss and this isn't a good sign. Not only will people resent working for him, but they will not respect him. Eventually this will make you dread going to work.

1. **Does your boss take the credit for things you did?** – This shows little empathy for his fellow workers. As long as the job is done, he doesn't recognize those who did it. Don't expect positive encouragement because the boss only gives this when he needs something.

1. **Do you suffer from depression?** – The chances are that your emotional intelligence is low if you do and that by increasing it, you can and will make positive changes to your life.

1. **Do you see the cup as half full or half empty?** – The chances are that if you are reading this book you are a little pessimistic toward life and you can change that by using emotional intelligence to up the positivity in your life and start believing in the half full cup.

1. **Do you find yourself anxious when you are not doing**

something? – Here, the problem is that you have not yet found peace within yourself. Thus, you are uncomfortable spending time alone and seek out the company of others or activities to hide this trait. Emotional intelligence will help you to get over it.

1. **Do you find it hard to relate to others?** – People with low emotional intelligence do have problems because they are too inward looking. Their expectations of others are too high and not at all compassionate.

1. **Do you depend upon others for validation?** – This is a sign of low emotional intelligence. In fact, you are so reliant upon others that you become a burden to them through constantly seeking approval and validation. Emotional intelligence, in this case, will help you to be less of a burden and more self-sufficient.
2. **Do you find you look back on the past a lot?** – People who do this miss out on what's happening now in their lives. They analyze life rather than living it.

1. **Do you find that you worry about the future?** – Again, people who spend all of their time worrying about the future don't spend much time in the moment they are in, thus losing opportunities to enjoy life to its fullest. Emotional intelligence helps them to be more present in their lives and that makes a huge difference to their perception of life.
2. **Do you find that you are not good in social situations and cannot read people?** – The problem here is that your esteem levels are already too low and thus, you find it hard to relate to others and worry about social interaction. Emotional intelligence helps you to come to terms with who you are and thus makes it easier to accept all kinds of social interaction.

1. **Do you panic when things go wrong?** – This is the perfect sign that your emotional intelligence needs to be increased. Emotionally intelligent people are able to pick themselves up and find another approach through their experiences and don't tend to look back on mistakes.

Apart from these obvious 12 signs of lack of emotional intelligence, there are others:

- *Lack of forgiveness of others*
- *Lack of forgiveness of self*
- *Lack of acceptance of self*

These can be put under the other headings, but I thought it relevant to mention them because unless you deal with these, you will always allow the above situations to happen to you and thus not display any kind of emotional intelligence because you can't forgive. Thus forgiveness needs to be high on your list of priorities.

If you see any of the above as being something that is relevant to your life, you need not worry. All of them will fade into obscurity once you start to grasp how emotional intelligence works and what it does for you. You may not believe it now, but as you go through the rest of this book, it is hoped that you can work on your emotional intelligence level so that you can cross these off your list of miseries! I did and I know that I was skeptical at first. Now that I have gained the emotional intelligence I once lacked, I decided to make this book to help others in situations that are similar to that which I accepted as the norm. It isn't. You can change it. All you need to do is take a new approach and the chapters that follow will show you how.

Can Emotional Intelligence be Learned?

It is common that people ask this question and the good news is that while some people have EQ as a natural talent, for those who don't, these skills can be learned. You see, people come from all kinds of backgrounds and these determine to a large extent how they approach their adult lives. You are taught by parents how to approach your life and some parents are more talented at this skill than others, so it follows that some kids with learn emotional intelligence from an early age, while others will find it harder to adjust their lives. You see, when you leave home as an adult, you already have set ideas and ideals in your mind, but life evolves and these change as you start to become an adult in the true sense of the word, making your own decisions. Those who have low emotional intelligence have never been shown how to react to life any differently, but there are different approaches that can increase their potential and it is these that they need to learn and understand in order to do that.

- **Self-awareness**
- **Self-regulation (managing emotions)**
- **Self-motivation**
- **Recognizing other emotions (empathy)**
- **Social skills**

These are the basics of emotional intelligence. So what do they mean in your life and how does emotional intelligence make a difference? In the next chapter you will find detailed information on 21 changes you can make in your life that will help you to increase your emotional intelligence. However, you need to see the benefits of learning before you actually approach doing it, so that you are going into this with your eyes open to the potential of success. In this chapter, you will learn how emotional intelligence applies to each of the above items.

Self-awareness – Do you really know who you are and what you want out of life? Are you happy with who you are? David felt that he wasn't that important in the order of things. He had a high IQ and could do most things, but socially he was inadequate. He thought that the problem lay with others, rather than himself. He was not aware of how others perceived him. He was unaware of his own body language and how awkward he appeared to others and why people were alienated by him. None of this was intentional, but by learning self-awareness, he was able to overcome the difficulties that his past had put in the way of making friends. By becoming aware of himself, he also started to like who he was and he learned that the more positive he felt about himself, the more positive others felt toward him. Self-awareness is where it all starts and to become self-aware, you use a series of exercises, such as meditation, journaling and observation to improve your level of emotional understanding of yourself.

Self-regulation – In this case, you are not emotionally aware of why you lose your temper, why you blame others and why your emotions take control of your approach to life. These emotions needs to be harnessed in some way. In the case of William, he lost his temper on a regular basis. Life seemed to be against him. However, when he talked about his problems much of this stemmed from inner frustration and lack of patience on his part. Through meditation and counseling, he was able to get back on track. You may not need counseling, but if you can learn about the triggers that put you into this state, it puts you in a better position to examine different reactions to those triggers and that's when you start to let emotional intelligence help you to self-regulate.

Self-motivation – Some people use others as crutches for their lives. Polly achieved what she did because she lived off the praise of others, but this isn't a very emotionally intelligent approach to life. Learning about mindfulness, she suddenly realized that what she craved from others could be found within her own mind. The self-motivation was there, but she had not tapped into it because she had not known how to do that. Mindfulness made her more aware that her own assessment of her performance was more relevant than the assessment made by people outside of self. When she learned that, she did it through goal setting and reward. This is a good way to move forward and to use emotional intelligence to achieve. She also learned to understand others and emotional intelligence showed her how others thought, how others reacted to her and indeed it was a shock to learn that she had lacked so much self-motivation that she had been a burden to people around her in her search for approval. Many people do this and get stuck into a vicious circle of needing validation from others to gain the energy to actually self-motivate, but when she learned self-motivation, her life changed considerably for the better.

Recognizing the emotions of others – We are often so filled with our own emotional feelings and thoughts that we don't take account of the feelings of others. We slam our way through life and wonder why other people don't understand us. When Susan took a course in mindfulness, she was shocked at what she found out about herself. All of her life she had placed judgment on people. It was them who had done things wrong. It was them who had rejected her ideas, but by closing off her mind to the thoughts and ideas of others and using them to blame for her own lack of empathy, she was not using emotional intelligence.

Mindfulness is a great remedy for this as well because it teaches you to be empathetic or to be able to put yourself into someone else's shoes and come up with solutions that not only suit self, but that will work in conjunction with others. That made her more productive, less negative and much more people friendly.

Social skills – Having tackled the rest, social skills are a walk in the park. Just like I said about my life, I had never really stopped to look beyond the surface and was incapable of reading people. When

I stopped blaming people for bad things that happened in my life, it opened up a whole new realm of potential in my life and I believe it is for this reason that I am driven to write this book in the first place. It is astounding the difference in my life and I want you to have an equal opportunity to open up avenues toward happiness in your life as well. If you are now ready, take on the next chapter, but have something ready to note down your intentions, so that these actually take place rather than just being intentions that never go anywhere.

21 Effective Steps to Increase EQ in Your Daily Life

In this chapter you will learn what it takes to increase your EQ and by the end of the chapter, you should be able to put these actions into motion.

1. **Learning to listen**

This is an important part of emotional intelligence because when you learn to listen you give other people a chance to air their views, but active listening is more than just listening to words. You can read the person in a better way when you stop and listen and will have a better handle on what makes that person tick. This also gives you a chance to think about your answers, rather than giving opinion too quickly and regretting it later.

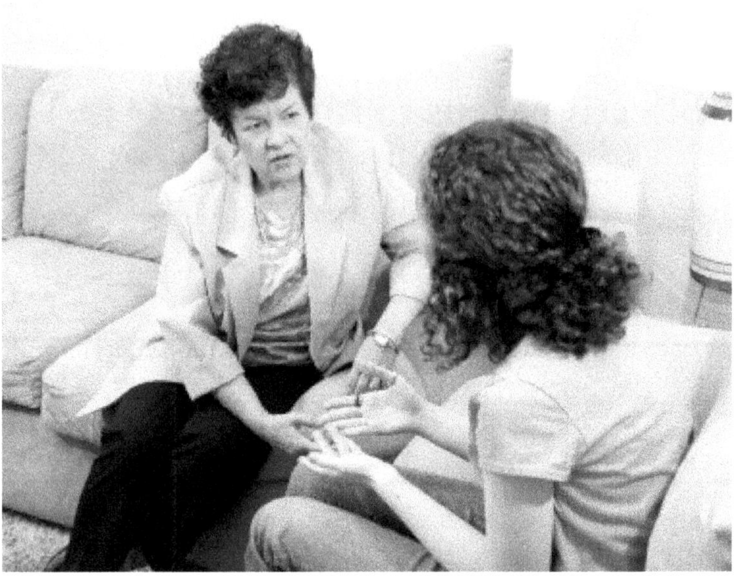

1. **Learning not to judge**

This is a harder one. When you learn meditation and mindfulness it becomes easier. The reason why your emotional intelligence is lower is because you haven't yet learned to stop judging situations. People make instant judgments and can sometimes be wrong. I thought, for example, that the girl at the party didn't want to know and wasted a lot of my time that could have been spent on getting to know her. You probably notice yourself doing things like this as well. Judgment creates negative thinking patterns. We judge people based on social expectations and may say "She is fat" or "He is not interesting" and we may even use judgment inwardly judging ourselves against set measures. It's time to realize that each individual human being has a reason for their actions and it's not your place to question them, but to accept that this is an individual right. If you want to be taken seriously in life and you want to gain more control over your emotions, this step will be a huge step in the right direction.

1. **Learn to meditate**

You may argue that you don't have time to meditate or that it's too complex. If you did watch the video by the neurosurgeon that was pointed to earlier in the book, you will know that her profession made her skeptical about mindfulness and meditation, but that she witnessed changes in her approach toward life that made her more compassionate and understanding of others and self. She began to see a person emerge who was more compassionate and who could use empathy in the place of apathy. It enriched her life. To meditate isn't as complex as you may imagine. All you need to do is put aside 15 minutes a day and if that means setting your alarm clock earlier, it will have been worthwhile because if you can make meditation a daily habit, you gain more from it. Sit in a hard chair with your back straight. The energy flow within the body works its way through the spine, so posture is everything. Close your eyes and make sure that you are in comfortable clothing and place your feet flat on the floor. Now, breathe in through the nostrils to the count of eight and then out to the count of ten and keep breathing in this way until your breathing forms a rhythm. When it does, start to go with that rhythm and be in this moment. That means that all of the things from the past are of no consequence and that things you have in your future are not to be thought about. Be in the breath. It's only fifteen minutes a day every morning before breakfast and the change that it will make in your life is astounding. As thoughts go through your mind, learn to dismiss them. Acknowledge them of course, because they are valid thoughts. They are simply not needed during the 15 minutes that you meditate, so let go of them. If you keep thinking, you will probably think you have failed, but it doesn't work like that. You simply kick those thoughts to one side and go on breathing and letting go of thoughts. That fifteen minutes can make a whole heap of difference to your emotional intelligence because you learn who you are. That may sound a little weird, but most people really don't spend that quiet time with themselves and don't let the subconscious mind rest enough to power them up to face the world and that's what meditation does. It allows them that freedom from thought and little by little, you find that it changes your whole perspective on life. When you know yourself better, you actually find acceptance much easier to incorporate into your life and that's amazing.

The other things that meditation will help you with is your heartbeat rate and your blood pressure and when you have finished, although you may not feel different straightaway, after practicing meditation over a prolonged period of time, you will find that you are able to concentrate more and that you don't let your emotions rule the roost. Instead, you have a clearer mind and are able to make decisions without the brain fog that you may have experienced in the past.

1. Learn to appreciate the moment

This is what mindfulness is all about. For example, how often do you eat your food without even noticing the taste or chewing the food correctly? What does that have to do with emotional intelligence? Well, the fact is that you are able to digest your food better and will not suffer from many of the ailments that are irritating, such as gut ache or even constipation. The stomach is a huge part of you and treating it well will help you to think more positive thoughts. You will also be able to use mindfulness to step into the moment whenever you are faced with things that are difficult for your emotions to handle. What you are doing is turning negative thought patterns into patterns that look at the moment that you are in. Instead of walking through a park thinking about the argument you had with your boss, you replace those thoughts with observations of what's happening right now. For example, you will see the plants and the seasons. You will notice things that perhaps you didn't notice before because you are being mindful of the walk and the place that you are visiting. Bringing your mind into the present moment is a way to change the habits of a lifetime. You can cull those negative thoughts and replace them with very positive ones, which will change your outlook toward life entirely. Mindfulness also slows down the process of the emotional responses that you have to live so that you are able to observe problems and cut out judgment of people and situations. Emotionally intelligent people are more versatile for a very good reason. They cut out all of the unnecessary judgment that others experience and free their minds of negativity by seeing all of the good things instead of the bad things. They also learn to drop judgment and can accept life more readily, making them less likely to make emotional mistakes. If there are mindfulness classes near you, then do take them because mindfulness helps to make you a much more compassionate person and more compassionate even toward yourself. You forgive things that happen and accept the bad with the good, but don't allow it to hold you back from thinking about positive solutions. You use all of your senses more and are able to distinguish the aromas of the world, the sights that you see and the emotional high that you get from opening your eyes and your senses to the world around you, taking any negative judgment out of the picture. This takes practice as we have already explained the amount of negative reactions people have to events that take place in their lives. Think of mindfulness as a steppingstone toward liberation from negative thinking patterns and you will start to enjoy your life more. For example, stop when you are eating and taste every texture and taste by chewing your food and concentrating on eating. Be aware of people around you and of the good things in the world, rather than letting your mind become myopic and negative thinking. Mindfulness also helps you to know yourself better and to better relate to the world around you, so will benefit you in so many different ways, including upping your ability to use emotional intelligence.

1. **Learn to prioritize**

The idea of prioritizing is to help you to overcome the potential of becoming emotionally overwhelmed by life. The problem is that you only have a set amount of hours in any day. If you try to fit everything into that time willy-nilly, you get to the stage where your emotions stop you from actually getting anything done at all. Thus, you need to be able to control that by knowing which tasks you need to do first and which can wait for another time. When you learn to prioritize you also have your head screwed on the right way and know that low priority jobs don't really matter that much in the order of things.

1. **Turn off negative influence**

When you look at people's Facebook pages, what you see is not a real world. Instead, you see what people want you to see. From drama queens all the way through to those who make you feel bad about yourself; they are all lined up ready to play with your emotions. It's time to learn when to cut off social media and it may even be a good idea to make Facebook a real place where the only friends you have are positive influences in your life. That way, you don't get emotionally sidetracked by stories that may or may not be real. So many people are putting themselves on display on these social media sites and what you see may not actually be what you think you see. Pictures get retouched, and you can even make yourself look slimmer by adjusting the photographs. Stop measuring yourself by these standards and start to be real about your life.

1. **Learn to delegate and share**

How does this help you? It helps you in your observation of others and helps to meet their needs to belong, instead of trying to inflate your worth and living with the emotional burden of doing so. Sharing your work with those who are around you shows a higher level of emotional intelligence. If you get stuck on something, ask someone who knows so that you will not be stuck next time. There are always people in the world who know more than you do about one particular aspect of your work, so don't feel that it demeans who you are. If you don't ask, this shows you to be lacking in understanding and unable to work with other people and you will never be chosen as potential promotion material.

1. **Minimize**

What does this mean? Madelaine used to put a great deal of value on the things that she owned. It was always a case of one-upmanship. She had learned this awful trait during high school, but as she got older, she suddenly found herself questioning her motives. Did anyone really care if her car was better than that of the neighbor? What about her home? Was it providing her with the comfort and peace that she was seeking? The fact was that it cost a lot of time to keep up with everyone else and many of the things she had purchased to impress others cost her dearly and were little used. When she stumbled upon the idea of minimalism, she had always thought that this meant some kind of deprivation, but following trends, she decided to give it a go. When you get rid of the clutter of things in your life, you simplify your life and find that your emotional levels are easier to handle. You are using emotional intelligence to understand that things don't buy happiness, but that this is something that should come from inside you, rather than be reflected by the number of things you own. As she decluttered her life, she found that she made more friends and that these were friends who accepted her for who she was. She also found that she liked herself more because she wasn't trying to compete and was happier with who she was. When you take away all of this bias from your life, you have room to be emotionally intelligent and to use your time in a better way, taking positive moves when it comes to sharing your time with others.

1. **Exercise and fresh air**

You may think this doesn't matter much when it comes to emotional intelligence, but you would be wrong. Even if all of the exercise that you get is a walk in the park every evening with the dog, it's a big step in the right direction. Why? Being in a natural environment helps you to think positively and to surround yourself with positive things. You notice the changes of the seasons, and the walk is also energizing your body and mind at the same time. People who do exercise frequently suffer less from emotional lows and are able to use that additional energy in a positive way. Erick never went walking. By the time he came home from the office, he was too tired, or that's the way he saw it. However, when they got a dog, he found that the walk in the evenings actually slowed his mind down so that he had more energy to use on the time that he did spend with his family and that this walking reduced his level of emotional strain, thus increasing his emotional intelligence and being able to relate more to people around him.

1. **Minimizing Negative influences**

This was a no brainer for Eleanor although she didn't see it at first. She surrounded herself with people who were either jealous of her or who used her. She allowed herself to be used and this had an impact on her self-esteem. She noticed one day that she wasn't coping well with being on her own, and thus didn't mind being used as a doormat because that was better than nothing. However, when she examined the relationships that she had in her life, she found that there were positive relationships as well as negative ones and that more and more she was spending time with people who made her feel negative. Stopping that spiral, she decided that unless people made her feel good about being herself, she had no room for them in her life. She cut down on the negative influences and became much more positive and proactive. This upped her self-esteem and also helped her to use her emotional intelligence to make her life a happier place to be.

1. **Journaling and positivity**

You may think that life is not offering you much, but how often have you tried to write down the positive things that you have to be grateful for? The chances are that these things happen without even being acknowledged. When you sit to eat your dinner, do you think of those who never have food to sit down to? What about when you wake up in the morning in a warm bed? Do you think of people who don't have that luxury? The problem is that we tend to err on the side of negative thought. No matter what you have, you may be yearning more without actually appreciating what you have. When you diary your gratitude toward life, you turn negative thought patterns into positive ones. If you ever watched the movie "Pollyanna", the main character was a little crippled girl. Her idea in life to overcome her handicaps was to see a positive light in every situation, and it affected all of the people around her. That's nothing new, but if you don't feel gratitude for those things that are right in your life, how will you ever be able to use emotional intelligence to pay it forward?

1. **Relaxation**

Often people do not take enough time to relax. This may mean that their minds are working overtime and that they are unable to see beyond how busy they are. Relaxation classes help and if you don't have time for classes, at least do a body scan when you find that your mind is overactive. This helps you to sleep and emotionally intelligent people know that the body needs time to sleep and relax so that all of the hormones that circulate in the body are able to do their healing. Lie down on a bed and lie on your back. It's best to do this in an atmosphere that is darkened, so close the drapes. You need one pillow only so that your airways are freed up. Close your eyes, breathe in through your nostrils and as you do so, start by thinking of your toes. Wiggle them and then relax them feeling them get heavier. You work your way up your body thinking of parts of your body and then tensing them and relaxing them until you are completely relaxed. Bear in mind that this will lower your blood pressure and heartbeat so don't try getting up straight away afterward. If you find that thoughts come into your mind, go back to your toes and concentrate on what you are doing. How does this help emotional intelligence? If your body and mind are too stressed, you tend to make snap judgments without really being able to digest what is happening. If you are rested, you are able to give more to your life and receive so much more in return. Your mental anguish is lowered, meaning that you are less responsive to negative emotions.

1. **Eating healthy foods**

Emotionally intelligent people usually eat the right kinds of foods. This is important because the body functions in a certain way given the fuel that it is fed. If you insist on eating snacks and packet foods, your body isn't getting the goodness it needs and chances are that you are overweight. This impedes your ability to love yourself and you may have self-esteem issues. Eating healthily will help you to overcome these issues.

1. **Volunteerism**

This is a very important change in your life because it helps you to boost your own self-esteem and stop relying upon others to boost it. If you are one of those people who is always seeking approval or validation from others, you need to learn that self-validation is much more important. Value yourself. Volunteer to help someone without any strings attached. Jennifer was always doing things to gain approval from others and when she didn't get that validation, she felt that she was not important enough. By finding a job at weekends at the local dog shelter, she found a great joy in giving her time to help out with feeding the dogs and exercising them and didn't need anyone to validate her. She was doing something for no thanks, as were the other volunteers, but it made her feel that she had value. That improved her self-esteem and an improvement in self-esteem equals the ability to control emotions and observe them so that you are more capable of upping your emotional intelligence in the process.

1. **Observation**

This helps you considerably to let go of pre-existing ideas. You may find that you are influenced by society into laying judgment on certain types of people. This exercise helps to show you how false those judgments are. Go to a mall and observe people. Write down the different types of people and then look to see what behavior someone exhibits that makes them:

- *Confident*
- *Attractive*
- *Friendly*
- *Positive*

Then contrast that with people who give off negative vibes. Write down the behaviors that give them negative vibes. You are learning about the way in which total strangers behave, but you are doing more than that. You are also giving yourself a chance to change. You are also giving yourself a chance to change your approach to life by taking on those traits that give the impression of confidence, friendliness, and positivity instead of any negative traits that are immediately given away by your posture.

1. Body Language

In the last exercise you looked at basic body energy. Now I want you to observe even closer. This could be with friends or family members to recognize things that are given across by negative thought processes. Use a mirror and examine your own body language. This helps to make you more emotionally intelligent because you are beginning to notice:

- *Eye movements*
- *The movement of the lips*
- *The sincerity of the smile*
- *The sarcasm*
- *The wit*
- *Mockery*

If you are able to read people in a better way, this helps you to interact with them better because you are aware of their weaknesses and strengths and are able to take these into account. Anthony used this when he was interviewing people for a job. Instead of basing the interviews on academic achievement, he based them on emotional response to questions and used his emotional intelligence to give him the instinct to use wisdom when choosing the right candidate. Understanding body language also enables you to gauge when it's the right time to make an approach or to suggest new things and with that knowledge, you become much more capable of success in your life and will know whether people around you are genuine or not.

1. **Improved social awareness**

This is achieved by being more interactive with the world around you and the easiest way to demonstrate this is for you to walk down the street with your head held high and smile when you pass people. It sounds like a kid's game or something that won't make much difference to your world, but it's amazing the difference it makes. When you approach the world with your head down and a grimace on your face, you add no joy either to your life or to the lives of people around you. By being more socially aware and taking in what's happening in your life rather than simply walking through life with no social awareness, you open yourself to possibility and use more emotional intelligence because you will find the world reacts with you in a more positive way as well.

1. **Be aware of positive behavior**

You may find this a very strange thing to say, but if you are not aware of the positive things that are happening around you, you lack empathy. The girl who brings you a cup of coffee daily does so because it's her job. It's a lowly job and not the best job in the world to have but let's face it, someone has to do it. Similarly, do you think that the road sweeper likes what he does? What about the office cleaner? Each of these people is equal to you as a human being and merits positive response to the small tasks that they do. In Buddhism, you are taught to do things or comport yourself in a manner that encourages others in their lives and helps to make them happier. Although you may not appreciate having to do this until you do, you are unable to really embrace empathy in your life and that's important. There's nothing wrong with thanking the girl for the coffee and showing appreciation for the small gestures made by people around you to make your world a better place. Empathy doesn't come from not observing. It doesn't come from ignoring that everyone else's world turns in the same way that yours does. It comes from understanding that everyone is playing a small part in a bigger picture.

1. **Getting close up with nature**

This is something that we all need to do more of. We don't scale the hills to look across the mountains that often. But if you live in a region where there is scenery that is awe inspiring or know somewhere like that, take advantage of it to help you to understand humility. It could be a beach at sunset or sunrise, but it will be somewhere that fills you with hope and gratitude and that actually makes you feel small. Why would you want to feel small? When I visited the Himalayas, I understood the concept of this totally for the first time in my life. It doesn't matter what your religious affiliation is. What matters is that you are aware that you have a spirit within you that is capable of being spiritual. This is the part of us that is the central core to our existence and you get pretty close to understanding it when you meditate daily, but never as quickly as you do when faced by the beauty of nature. Standing on the top of my favorite hill, I am reminded about how small I am in the order of things, and that increases your emotional awareness and your ability to use emotional intelligence to see in front of you what's real and what's not real. The fact that the world is made up of small elements and that the beauty depends upon even the smallest grain of sand helps you to feel something inside that allows you to experience humility. When you start at this base level, everything that you feel in life is heightened and you can share this through using emotional intelligence with your relationships, your reactions to people and your ability to take on even the smallest of tasks. It improves who you are and the scene that you observe helps to increase your gratitude.

1. **Learning about emotions**

It helps you considerably to learn about positive emotions. Learn by observation of yourself. Learn what makes you angry and why. Learn what makes you feel negative feelings and examine why these happen. When you are able to do that and draw it out onto a piece of paper, then apply the fact that you are stepping away from judgment. Mindfulness will help you to do this, but you first need to examine what it is that makes you emotionally stunted. Each bias that you have and each prejudice that you experience stunts your emotional growth, so if you can journal what they are and then work on eliminating them from your life, you are in a better position to increase your emotional intelligence. Let me demonstrate this. Geoff was always made to feel small when he was with his family. This was something he kept feeling most of his life until the day his father died and the family gathered to say goodbye to him. He had spent most of his life being jealous of his sister, who seemed to have a natural talent in passing exams and showing the perfect example and his father had reminded him of this all of his life. When he spoke to her, he later examined the conversation. Not only was she made totally miserable by her father using her as the measurement of goodness, but it had stunted her enjoyment of life. She felt negative toward her brother because he had all of the freedom she had never had the luxury to experience. Much of the time, our biases and our prejudices are ill founded. In their later lives, Geoff and his sister were able to make peace with each other and actually enjoyed each other's company, both now understanding how wrong their perceptions had been all of their lives. Using emotional intelligence to examine your biases helps you to overcome them. Taking judgment out of your life also helps you to examine things as they are, rather than how you perceive them to be, as often what we perceive is one pointed and myopic. Your emotional intelligence takes a huge boost when you drop judgment and start living your life according to your own happiness levels, rather than being an underdog or trying to live your life in a superior way to impress people. When you cut out the emotional factor from the way you approach life and simply enjoy it for what it is in this moment, it becomes a lot more giving and you become more valuable as a human being.

1. **Learning to let go**

I left this until last for a very good reason. It's one of the most difficult hurdles to overcome when you are trying to improve your emotional intelligence. Letting go means forgiving yourself for your mistakes and learning by them. It also means letting go of blame. Blame is only a part of your life because you allow it to be and most people don't intentionally cause harm. Blame is counter-productive and instead of helping your emotional intelligence, actually stops it in its tracks. Write down all of the things you feel that you need to forgive yourself and others for. Then actively take one at a time and let go of the problem by addressing it and forgiving those involved so that you are able to feel the weight of that problem dissipate. When you do this, you will find that the load in your life becomes much lighter. "How can I forgive someone who does this?" asks one person. "How can I forgive that kind of behavior?" asks another. The fact is that if someone's behavior made you feel that you could never forgive them, they have won. They have defeated you. They are taking your emotional intelligence and screwing it into a ball so tight, you can't get out of it. You blame them. You blame someone else, but in fact when you are able to forgive and move on, your emotional intelligence takes a huge boost and you become more compassionate, both with yourself and with others. We can never really know what makes people do the things that they do. Some of the biggest mistakes of our lives may have been initially caused by others, but if we make the mistake of letting those mistakes break us, then we are as guilty as the offender because we go forward with a broken spirit and a broken life. That's why letting go is the most important thing that you can do, in order to take back control of your emotional intelligence.

Over the course of this chapter, there was a lot of activity and it won't all happen at once. You need to take one of the standpoints at a time and work on that until you are satisfied that it has made a difference in your life. Then move on to the next standpoint and work that into your life. It doesn't have to take forever and if you indeed learn to incorporate mindfulness and meditation into your life, then forgiveness and the ability to listen to your body and your instincts will also improve. Your emotional growth depends upon it and your emotional intelligence will improve with each step that you take toward that eventual goal of happiness and success.

Conclusion

I am very glad that you got this far with the book because that means that you have a better idea about what emotional intelligence is all about. You also have the tools to use it to improve your life. It took me a long time to realize and appreciate that I control how happy and successful my life is. In fact, I would say it took too long, considering that I could have used that emotional intelligence earlier in my life and had more of this happiness that I experience now every day from the moment that I wake up. Life offers us a series of experiences. Some see that cup overflowing while others are lucky to scrape the bottom of the cup, but it's not because there's nothing in the cup to enjoy. It's because they don't have the foresight to actually realize how full that cup really is.

The next time that you look at yourself in the mirror look at your eyes. They tell you a lot about your happiness level. Do they smile? Do they look skeptical? Do they look suspicious of life? Now smile and look at how that smile radiates across your face. However, realize that unless it's a genuine smile, it won't go near the wrinkles under your eyes and you won't feel that energy that true happiness brings into your life. Emotional intelligence is a shared thing. It's the way you interact to the world around you and how you receive the messages that form part of what your life becomes.

You will have learned from the book how to change your view toward the things that happen in your life, to learn by them and to help all the bad things that happen to make you grow emotionally. No one will pretend that it's easy, but the stronger you make yourself now when things are going relatively well, the easier you will find the road when bad things happen. Emotional intelligence covers so many areas of your life as I have explained in the chapters of this book and if this makes a difference to the lives of only a few readers, it will have been worth the journey.

Don't expect to "get it" straight away. We have the ability to grow our emotional intelligence, but it takes time for this to happen. However, if you really do want it to happen, nothing should stop you now that you know the route that takes you there. I have given you a lot of food for thought and a lot of evidence from professionals in the field of neuroscience and psychology and all of this points to the fact that EQ can be changed, but IQ is something you were born with. With more and more employers understanding the difference, watch out for those emotional based questions at interview because they will certainly trip up those who are not emotionally aware. Those who will win the day because it takes more than brains to become successful. Brains and emotional intelligence will be the perfect combination to help you in all areas of your life including friendships, relationships and work oriented contact with other people, as well as the ability to enjoy your singularity as an individual.

I leave you with a quotation from Daniel Goleman 0n emotional intelligence which should make you want to go back to the tips and strategies in this book and start putting them into action in your life:

"What really matters for success, character, happiness and lifelong achievements is a definite set of emotional skills – your EQ — not just purely cognitive abilities that are measured by conventional IQ tests." —
Daniel Goleman

The Top 10 Essential Oils For Anxiety

Do you feel anxious when faced with a problem at work, when you have big events or before taking a test?

Looking for ways to manage anxiety?

Stress and anxiety have become common issues in our fast-paced lives...

This has a negative impact on our health both mentally and physically.

But did you know that there are certain essential oils that have huge benefits when it comes to relieving anxiety and stress?

To discover the top 10 essential oils for anxiety, visit: https://bit.ly/2xLD2Yb

Resources

https://www.scientificamerican.com/article/feeling-our-emotions/[1]

https://www.bbc.com/news/world-us-canada-12661646

https://www.inc.com/marcel-schwantes/how-do-you-know-a-job-candidate-has-true-emotional.html

1. https://www.scientificamerican.com/article/feeling-our-emotions/

EMPATH

An Extensive Guide For Developing Your Gift Of Intuition To Thrive In Life

Alison L. Alverson

Introduction

Greetings readers! Congratulations for taking the first step towards transforming your life. My understanding of what an empath is became substantial and real while I was in Mexico. I was a primary school teacher in Veracruz, for a UNICEF All-in-school initiative. This rural and rugged neighborhood was predominated by aggressive Latinos and a dislike for foreigners. The education and social system in that part of North America was quite strange for an American like me. I took great interest in the academic wellbeing of the students, often to a fault.

Maria had been absent from school for about two weeks and, as her class teacher, I was worried. Alicia struck me as a mother who was very concerned about her daughter's education. So, I went to visit the young child. Every Latino brow was raised at me, as I walked down the local neighborhood of Juarez. My presence as an American was a threat to everyone around me. It was actually a bit of irritation and a lot of anger. "TEE-chuch" Maria shouted as she ran towards me. Then Alicia joined us, and she had a very surprised look.

With barely a short conversation, she hurriedly agreed to bring her child to school the next day. The tension in her response seemed like something wasn't right and I wasn't in the right environment to question her. It seemed like she was scared that someone would find an American with her in such a neighborhood. The next day, I was in front of the blackboard teaching the students - including Maria. All of a sudden, there was a disturbing rant that caught my attention. I went out of the class to check and just at the door, Alicia walked briskly into the class with her face bruised to a pulp.

Alicia grabbed her daughter's arm and dragged her out of the class. Just before she exited, she hissed at me. I watch the two strolls down the stairs. Not long after, there was a gunshot as Alicia held her daughter closer, clueless of which direction to move on the stairs. A pickup van drove to a stop at the side of the building. Two armed men jumped out and came up the stairs. I went back into the class to check on the students, but they looked unthreatened. The bandits had been invading schools and churches frequently. Alicia ran into the class and asked me to go into hiding. Before she could explain the rationale, the Mexican bandits came into the class, "Where is the American?" At this point, there were too many questions running through my head, and I am sure you can imagine some of them. From my ironed tie to the spotless long sleeves, I was obviously the American that they were looking for. One of the armed guys pointed a gun at me with so much disgust, as if I had offended him. "Your president keeps harassing us" he said in an irate way. As he was about to shoot, Alicia jumped in front of me, knelt on the floor and started begging like her life was at stake.

How could I have begged the angry Mexican if it had not been for Alicia? She endangered her life just to protect me. She forgot the presence of her child or the other students and fought for an American. Despite the stained profile attached to Americans in that part of the Mexican city, she stood up for me. Alicia was not brave; she was not a superhero; she was only an empath. An empath is someone who can absorb other people's emotions and sometimes suffer physical symptoms due to their high sensitivity.

They develop a natural connection with absorbed emotions, and they respond appropriately. It was my experiences in Mexico with Alicia that motivated this literary expression of an empath's claim and who an empath is. The book gives an extensive overview of the characteristics and traits of empaths with Alicia as a case study. This series also addresses imaginative questions like, "What if Alicia was shot? Was her action brave?" Where should the line between been an empath and been logical be drawn? Should the line even exist? This page thriller consistently connects the inferred theories about empaths with my real-life account. At the end of this series, readers should be able to identify empaths.

This won't be that difficult as about 2 – 4% of the American population is clairsentience; a group that covers empaths. A lot of similar exercises are included in this series for a comprehensive understanding including the discussion of the causative agents of this extreme level of sensitivity. So let's dive in!

Introduction to Being an Empath

Who is an empath?

An empath is a person who is deeply sensitive to the emotions and situations of those around them. This sensitivity is often to a level where they feel the emotions themselves, equipping them with the capacity to respond appropriately. Their keen interest in interacting with the emotional needs of others makes them very understanding. If the connection is deep enough, empaths can feel someone else's pains. This chapter discusses what an empath is, the traits common to an empath and how people become empaths. This connection is not restricted to humans alone as some other types of empaths interact with the needs of animals, plants, places, the environment etc.

What are the traits common to empaths?

These characteristics differentiate them from Highly Sensitive People (HSP) who just have great empathy. Irrespective of the several types of empaths they all share some common traits. Here are some of the attributes common to empaths.

- **Heightened sensitivity**: This is the most common and basic trait of empaths. They tend to pick up on the feelings and thoughts of others, no matter how hidden. Empaths react and connect to these emotions like they are the subjects. This high level of sensitivity can be related to mirror neurons. Scientists theorize that these neurons read emotional cues from others and connect to their thoughts.

The subtle changes in expressions, body language, and other parameters are easily noticeable by empaths. Most times these small changes are often another form of more delicate circumstances. Plant empaths can connect, understand and communicate with plants as even the most subtle organisms have things to say. The nature of plants would obviously infer that their communication is very latent. It requires extreme sensitivity to relate to the little movements of leaves and branches.

- **Overwhelming emotions***:* This sensitivity can also be unintentional as it also occurs in public places. The nature of empaths leaves them vulnerable to every type of emotion. The numerous and contrasting ambiance of crowds and noisy environments can be challenging. In effect, empaths react and respond to the nature of their environments. Empaths become more effectively sensitive in quiet and serene surroundings. They internalize these feelings and respond respectively. Plant empaths often get irritated with human activities that alter or compromise the wellbeing of trees and plants. This ends up creating overwhelming emotions especially because there is very little that can be done about it. Geomantic empaths are certainly not left out. Imagine a geomantic empath that has developed a deep bond and connection with the ocean witnessing the ocean littered with plastic bottles and waste. This is common with countries that share the ocean's coastline. In some parts of Africa, the drainage and sewage system all lead into the ocean. The sight of this environmental discrimination can overly dampen the feelings and the emotions of geomantic empaths.

- **A grounded understanding of other's emotions***:* One of the core traits of an empath is the ability to understand the origin of people's emotions. This understanding creates a natural connection with others. Empaths know the other party's thoughts and feelings even when they are finding it hard to express them. In such a case, empaths even help others articulate and express themselves better. An animal empath can deduce that when fleas are hovering over a dog, then a disease could be contracted. The connection they share with the animals gives them the capacity to understand and interpret every little behavior properly.

- **Useful and relevant advice***:* The insights and genuine characteristics of empaths are why they are always sought after for advice and emotional support. In the course of this, empaths tend to be good listeners, willing to hear all the complex emotions. The relevant advice provided by empaths is a reflection of their understanding of other people's emotions. Emotional empaths connect with absorbed emotions but remain mentally stable enough to react appropriately or give objective and relevant solutions. Most deforesters really do not understand the negative consequence of their activities. A lot of them see deforestation as the only alternative but with the grounded understanding of an empath, relevant and resolving advice or alternatives can be offered. There is a general problem of lack of information and can be solved with relevant advice.

- **Calm and non-violent nature**: As mentioned earlier, empaths function better in a quiet and calm environment. These factors are internalized and make them easily irritated by violence. This irritation also translates into movies as they can't watch violent movies. They respond positively to calm environments and negatively to violence. It is almost impossible to find a geomantic empath that has a deep connection with disorderly and crowded places like the marketplace. This is because their subtle and sensitive nature ensures that they are only able to connect and process orderly stimuli and emotions. An Empath's vacation is most likely to be spent at the beach on a quiet day or in an isolated island. They can travel over land and watch the elephants in African game reserves. Others even spend their holidays in solitude or alone.

- **Love for pets and babies***:* The pure nature of animals and babies easily appeals to the genuineness of empaths. They find it easier to appreciate and connect with pets and babies. This connection is a result of the genuineness of both parties. This is not just peculiar to animal empaths as all the types of empaths share a genuine nature and emotional purity. Hence their connection with babies and animals is natural. It is also important that the connection and likeness goes both ways.

- **Complications in relationships***:* The constant closeness of empaths to someone else like a partner can be very challenging. These challenges are a result of the constant sensing of their partner's mood, irritation or feelings. The constant presence of a partner is a big drag on the empath's energy. This is even more so when the partner is very insensitive. Alicia was married to an emotionally passive man, in the person of Miguel. She takes on the burden of every emotional need. Without any form of support, she solely ensures the academic wellbeing of their daughter. Miguel discourages her nature and emotional tendencies, but she still has to care for him to maintain the required balance. Some empaths resort to staying single; others create a private room in their homes for just themselves.

- **Truthfulness**: The truthful and sensitive nature of empaths gives them the capacity to identify lies and truth. They are receptive to even the slightest social cues from others, so it is almost impossible to lie to them. This is obvious in the case of animal empaths as their nature is always true and genuine. Humans have the tendency to suppress their emotions and feelings, but empaths can always see beyond the external cues. Their developed intuitions overcome every form of emotional barrier.

- **Calming effect and emotional healing**: The connective and genuine nature of empaths makes it easy for others to open up to them. During trying times, people often seek their most empathetic friends, which is what empaths represent. The openness of others is the first step to emotional healing. The effect they have on others helps in resolving emotional baggage and unraveling unhealthy patterns. Because animal empaths understand and genuinely care, the animals tend to open up. These animals are violent to people that they cannot connect with. For example, the relationship between a dog and a dog owner becomes very affectionate over time. This is because the owner can now put meaning and interpretation to every behavioral change. The dog also gets to know the implication of every gesture of the owner. This is unlike the animal empath who gets all this connection and interaction with animals in just a moment. They do not require a very long time for the development of the connection.

- **Compassion**: Most empaths feel obligated to help people in need, without consideration of how this will come about. They place the utmost priority on helping others. They can stop every endeavor just to focus on someone else. When emotional empaths absorb the feelings of others, they don't understand everything in the instance. But they still take the risk knowing they might not be able to help. Alicia couldn't have been 100% sure that the Mexican bandit would not shoot but her compassion was hard to suppress. It is only compassion that would make plant empaths want to interact with the endangered species of plants and trees. It is safe to say that the first instinct of empaths is compassion; they go to the trouble of using their emotional energy and strength to make resolutions.

The Science of Being an Empath

The traits of empaths are closely linked with the mirror neuron system. This system in the brain enables empaths to feel the emotions of others. When empaths sense negative or sad emotions from others, the neurons in the brain become activated. The activation stimulates experiences corresponding to the ones the other person is going through. There are credible theories on empaths and how the evolution of intuition which might have resulted from biological and psychological uniqueness between empaths and others. There are several scientific theories that can explain the special attributes and behaviors of empaths.

- **Sensory Processing disorder**: This is a medical condition that makes a person struggle with processing absorbed information. The inability to properly use this input creates a magnified effect on every unit of information being absorbed. When the senses are over stimulated, they react in line with the nature of data. This can result in dizziness, anxiety or even confusion. The sensitivity is also present in the level of people's emotions. So, they are aware of the feelings of others. Some research links these traits to genetic components and others postulate that the disorder is due to abnormal brain activities. This anomaly can be in response to noise, light and other over-stimulating inputs. The disorder can also be as a result of the inability to process feelings and emotions. Alicia came to help plea for me. What if she did this because of her inability to process violence or even death? It is possible that she couldn't comprehend the situation and she acted from a faulty processing.

- **Overactive mirror neurons***:* Mirror neurons are brain cells with proven connection to human compassion. These neurons are basically responsible for empathy. Empaths tend to be sad when others are hurting or happy when others are. These mirror neurons can activate reactions corresponding to those of observed emotions. In a sense, this theory tries to take the control of emotions from the empaths. The neurons are just suggestive, and this comes in a very subtle nature. An empath can still decide to be happy when others are sad or at least positive emotions can still be practiced. Nonetheless, empaths often succumb to these neurons and react accordingly.

- **Electromagnetism***:* A lot of the symptoms and characteristics expressed by empaths can be explained by electromagnetism. The major question that the theory answers is if the electromagnetic field is capable of influencing the magnetic field of others. In this theory, the heart and the brain of empaths generate electromagnetic fields, which are interactive with the individual's feelings and emotions. With close emotional proximity, their energy fields interact, and information can be received, and emotions connected to. This explains the capacity of empaths to cash in on even the hidden emotions of others without deciding to. It also gives credence to the exhaustive feelings empaths suffer when in crowded and disorderly places. Their electromagnetic field interacts with so many diverse and sometimes contrasting emotions from others.

- **Hormones and chemical activities:** This theory links the level of sensitivity to hormonal levels and neuro-transmitters. The study was centered upon dopamine, a neurotransmitter that influences the human response to pleasure. The study revealed that empaths are more sensitive to dopamine than others. They require less of it to achieve pleasure. Empaths are more reactive to chemical changes in themselves and others. The little cues from the chemical changes in someone else is easily noticed and reacted to. Empaths possess a lower chemical threshold than most, so they tend to sense and react excessively. The study extensively covered dopamine but effective on most neuro-transmitters.

- **Emotion contagion***:* In this theory, emotions are just contagious. A baby has a high probability of crying when there is another baby crying. People who are subject to kindness often show kindness. It is a very simplistic way of explaining the complexity of empaths. They mirror the emotions around them, internalize them, and often react more rationally. This theory puts the nature of empaths at a disadvantage because to better society, empaths need to express superior emotions and behaviors. Society wouldn't be substantially improved by empaths if empaths are just reflective of a bad society. Geomantic empaths would naturally be happy at the beach because of the nature of the emotions expressed in such an environment. The lively and vacation like atmosphere would be reflected in the empath's emotions. On the other hand, if the geomantic empath is in crowded, toxic environments the emotions are most likely going to be negative.

- **Synesthesia***:* It is a medical condition that links two different traits which naturally wouldn't be connected. Individuals with synesthesia might link colors or songs. In the case of empaths, scientists believe mirror-touch synesthesia allows empaths to feel what others are feeling. In the experience, the empaths feel like the emotions are originating from them. The experiences and thoughts of the empath and the other person might not be connected but a link is derived. When Alicia saw me at gunpoint, she might have linked the scenario to a similar event in her past, which is unconnected to mine but brings out similar emotions. She connected the two experiences and effectively reacted like it was personal to her.

How does a person become an empath?

A lot of these traits were displayed by Alicia when she stuck out her neck for me. Obviously, she was driven by compassion to help an American stranger like me. She might have linked my situation to some experience in her past. She connected with it and reacted like her life was what was at stake. She also had an effective connection and communication with the bandit who surrendered to her plea. This had a calming effect on the raging Mexican who changed his mind. As an empath, she had the capacity to express my emotions appropriately while I stood in awe. Even after the men had left, she remained on the ground, wondering why she just risked her life for me. The tears might have also been as a result of her irritation towards violence. Alicia could have acted in contrast to her nature, but she would regret any consequence for the rest of her life. That emotional drag would last for a lifetime, which is incomparable to the temporary emotional drain she felt for standing up for me. There are several reasons why empaths exist in the world. The majority of these causes are temperament, genetics, trauma, and supportive parenting. **These are just psychological reasons as there are also scientific explanation for their existence and evolution:**

- **Temperament:** Some people are born with more sensitivity than others as some babies just have it when they are born. Some babies squint to the barest form of light, they cry when there are too many faces. The sensitivity of such babies evolves into the traits earlier ascribed to empaths. Geomantic empaths develop their passion and likeness for particular places and geographic sites from experiences. Their calm nature also cumulates into a natural tendency and attraction to quiet and serene places.

- **Genetics**: Some of these traits are genetically transmitted. Highly sensitive children often come from highly sensitive parents. This probability suggests the genetic influence on the traits. It is important to note that some of the traits are not inborn, they are developed. So even when empaths are born with the traits, they have to be developed or else they would end up just being empathetic. Since the traits have been related to mirror neurons, then there is a chance that is genetic.

- **Trauma**: Emotional or physical abuse can influence the extent of sensitivity of individuals. The influence is usually more extensive when the abuse is from the parents. A lot of empaths have alcoholic, depressed or narcissistic parents. This faulty parenting ironically leads to a lack of emotional defense and it creates a high level of selflessness. Their traumatic experiences are so evasive that they will always try to help others during trying times. They can easily relate other's predicaments to a traumatic event in their past. A person who lost a pet to illness or carelessness is likely to become an animal empath. There exists a natural tendency to remember the lost pet when there is a struggling pet around. This traumatic experience will ensure that the empath provides help in any way possible, because the first instinct towards animals is now compassion.

- **Supportive parenting:** These positive traits expressed by empaths can be effectively developed by good parenting. The traits and characteristics naturally evolve. Parents can direct and guide this behavioral evolution for better functioning. As earlier indicated, dysfunctional parenting can also develop this trait, but this type of empath often lacks a defined boundary. They are the ones that find it impossible to say no, even when they can't provide the solution. This is in contrast to the empaths whose traits are developed and functionally guided by the parents. They are like the trained empaths who can disconnect with absorbed emotions when necessary. Their emotional limits are established, and they observe the boundaries. Imagine having an environmentalist as a father with different forms of flowers and plants around the house, in the garden and on the veranda. Such a child would naturally develop a keen interest in gardens and plants. On the other hand, a person who becomes a plant empath as a result of disasters like ground erosion as a result of bush burning and deforestation are the kind of empaths who will go the extra mile to ensure the well-being of trees and plants.

Understanding the Type of Empaths and Their Methods of Emotional Security

Types of empath

There exist several types of empaths that can be basically classified into six. Other types that have been identified but are just similar variants of these primary ones. These different classifications are as a result of the various factors and complexities associated with the traits and empathic abilities of empaths:

- **Emotional empath**: This is one of the most common classes of empaths. They have the unconscious capacity to pick up on the emotions of others. The feelings of the people around them influence the mood and feelings of emotional empaths. This type of empath is not able to differentiate their emotions from those of others. A lot of times, this kind of empath ends up being drained often due to the emotional connection.

- **Physical/emotional empath**: This type of empath can connect with the energy of others. The depth of this physical interaction makes most of the empaths end up as healers (medical doctors or into alternative medicine). During treatment, the empaths have an awareness of the patient's body and pains. They develop symptoms from other's ailments, and they can sense blockage strains in their energy fields. This type of empath that ends up as medical doctors remain unsettled until patients are cured, and problems resolved.

- **Animal empaths**: The connection with animals is predominant amongst these empaths but at a subtle level. Only a few have very deep empathy towards animals. These animal empaths devote a lot of their time to taking care of pets and animals in general. They develop the capacity to communicate and understand the expressions of animals. When a cat winks, it is trying to express the need for affection; this is one of the many interactions that are understood by animal empaths. They know when the animal is sick, they understand every behavioral change in animals and their consequences.

- **Geomantic empaths**: Those with this type of empathy have a sound attunement with physical landscapes or occurrences. Geomantic empaths express different emotions and moods in different environments without any apparent reason. They develop deep connections to certain places and certain things like sacred stones and certain natural figurines. A healthy love for the environment and good treatment of it ensures that geomantic empaths show a great responsibility for the wellbeing of trees and other natural objects. As earlier discussed in chapter one, empaths often get depleted and they sometimes need to recharge their energy and empathy. For geomantic empaths, they recharge from nature, the landscape, the ambiance, and the serenity of their surroundings. These empaths often like to surround themselves with natural objects.

- **Plant empath**: Plant empaths are ones that have a natural passion for plants. They like to establish communication by spending time with plants. According to some plant empaths, they receive guidance from plants and trees. They are of the opinion that plants and trees have opinions, but their expressions require some level of connection and unconventional interaction. A lot of these types of empaths end up working in gardens, parks, or wild landscapes where their passion is put to good use.

- **Intuitive empaths:** These empaths are subconsciously receptive to the emotions of people around. A little time with others gives them so much insight and information. They have the capacity to read the intentions behind the expression of others. It is almost impossible for them to be lied to. A lot of these empaths end up as therapists where they can construct correct opinions and profiles about patients.

Nevertheless, some empaths are a combination of various types. For instance, Alicia showed the characteristics of both an emotional and a physical empath. She didn't react according to her emotions or feelings. She keyed into my emotional energy and reacted physically like I should have. I was overwhelmed by the situation and I couldn't have reacted rationally.

Empath's precaution

The vulnerable nature of the various types of empaths requires some precautionary measures on their part. This is because they can easily be disadvantaged by their genuine and selfless nature. If the bandit had shot her, then he would have also shot me. That would have made it a double loss situation for everyone. I wouldn't assume to be the one to draw the line between empathy and reasoning but here are some of the precautionary measures. **Precautions that should be observed by empaths to avoid been drained and taken advantaged of are as follows:**

- **Empath's sensitivity often draws them into others' emotions**. This can be very draining hence the need for empaths to differentiate between their emotions and those of others. There should be a line or boundary for the emotional interaction. Empaths should learn to safeguard their sensitivities. A physical empath should be able to isolate the pain of others. If they are mixed up, the reaction might not be as rational and objective as it should be. Alicia was able to isolate the emotions and feelings absorbed for me so that she made the bandit see reason. If my emotions had been mixed with hers, the plea might not have sounded like a defense for me. She might have just been begging, oblivious of the real reason for it.

- **For a lot of physical empaths, they develop health complications from being too connected and symptomatic to others' health problems**. The physical empaths need to enrich their energetic field and should undergo some form of training. Trained empaths know when to disconnect from the energy or emotions. Without training, a lot of these empaths become mentally and emotionally dampened. The truth is that this automatically reflects physically. An unhealthy state of mind will always affect one's physical health.

- **Empaths need to surround themselves with the right environment and people.** The right environment can help enrich and develop their traits. For example, geomantic empaths should acquaint themselves with the right physical landscape. Plant empaths should also stay around plants and trees to strengthen their energetic field. They should be around those they feel aligned with. Alicia stood a high chance of developing negative tendencies and addictions because of her partner. She was constantly entangled with the grievous and discriminating tendencies of her husband. She was always stressed by the emotional carelessness of Miguel, yet she felt obligated to remain helpful. Her circumstances cannot be separated from her neighborhood. A lot of the Mexicans in Juarez had the same outlook of being peasants, financially struggling yet egoistic. The biggest mistake that an empath can make is been surrounded by the wrong type of people.

- **Animal empaths spend a lot of time with animals and this interaction can easily be harmful**. A lot of studies (biological or psychological) and training can help ensure a proper and healthy relationship with animals. The compassion and the intuition that empaths live by need to be schooled. Especially for animals as a lot of diseases can be contracted from them if the necessary precautions are not taken. Training ensures that rational compassion becomes the first instinct and that the interaction observes the limits.

- **Quiet time is also an effective way for empaths to reenergize and revitalize their mental state.** Empaths do not have to do this in one place. They can take a walk, allow themselves a walk down the road or around the office. These interludes help to reposition the moods and nerves. Animal empaths typically have a lot of pets. A large part of their time is spent with animals. This necessitates some momentary time away from animals, maybe a vacation to an island or even the beach. This time spent without animals and noise helps to strengthen the emotions and improve the emotional perspective.

- **Meditation can help empaths centralize their energy.** This reduces emotional overload and ensures that empaths do not break down because of the emotions of others. In meditation, empaths are advised to escape from their active thoughts. The several minutes should be spent in complete devotion to quietness and nature. Meditation generally widens human perspective and places focus on the right path. The concept is similar to bush fallowing in agriculture where activities are halted at a farm to help it regain its value and nutrients. You can check my book CHAKRA HEALING FOR BEGINNERS to learn more about how to be in harmony through guided meditation.

How should empaths protect themselves? How should they maintain their emotional strength?

I call it a sudden twist of fate. The Mexican wanted to shoot and then he didn't. Alicia was convincing enough to save my life. After she and her daughter had left, the students stared at me, waiting for the rest of their teaching. I scrambled to the ground and told them all to go home. The sound of their back heeled sandals tethering against the concrete floor brought back my imagination. I imagined my ribs shattering in my body supposing the trigger had been pulled. After the dust of reality had settled, I needed to thank Alicia for saving my life. I didn't want to visit them, so I poured out my appreciations in a letter. Unfortunately, the husband got to the letter first and it seemed like an affectionate letter from an admirer. He called out his wife and angrily waited for an explanation.

Alicia took the letter and tried to explain that it was from Maria's teacher in school. He asked her for my name, but she didn't respond. He then called Maria and asked for her class teacher's name. She looked at Alicia in consideration as Miguel squeezed her daughter's mouth. He forced my name out her mouth as Miguel raged and she felt there was no choice. Alicia knew he would go looking for me, so Alicia pulled all resistance to revealing my identity to protect me. She was ready for any form of violence from her husband in defending me. She compromised and complicated the relationship with her husband for a stranger. In a real sense, she was just trying to avoid violence, which was a sure outcome, now that my identity was revealed. You might ask, how should Alicia have protected herself? But the more important question is who should Alicia be protected from? Empaths are usually calm and irritated by violent tendencies. So, the relationship of Alicia to her violent husband could only be wrong or demeaning to her nature. Empaths should protect themselves by avoiding close relationships with people who have contrasting characteristics. It's easy to think that Alicia should have picked the side of her husband in my stead, but empaths naturally gravitate towards emotional victims like me. If the empathetic nature is not satisfied, they tend to isolate themselves and exist in a very conservative and depressed mood. It is important to note that Alicia wasn't just receptive to my emotions, but she also understood what the Mexican bandit was feeling. The first words of the bandit were "Where is the American?" This suggested that they had no real knowledge of who I was, and they were projecting an anger toward me. From his latter words, they were obviously angry at the international policies of the American president. The vendetta wasn't personal or that deep. Alicia probably cashed in on this line of thought. She calmed his nerves with soothing Spanish words that re-aligned his thought with the reality of not solving anything through my death. However reasonable this sounds; it came with huge risks as the Mexican could have still decided to shoot us both.

I heard intruding knocks on the door. Someone burst through the door. It was Miguel. His eyes were red. He caught my arm and then he said, "Stay far away from my wife. If I see any other letter from you, you will be in trouble!" He then took his triumphant exit. I spend the rest of that hour thinking if I had made a bad choice leaving America. Miguel's rage was not completed as he went home to Alicia. He unleashed his violence on Alicia with slaps and punches. Her empathetic nature wouldn't let her react as she ran out of the house in tears. Not long after, I heard a knock on my door again and I grabbed a plank. I pulled the door ajar and staggered out with a plank in my hand. Alicia was shocked by the sight of me as my defensive position showed vulnerability. I dropped the plank and she asked if I was okay. Personally, I believe empaths should not run from their nature. They should actually embrace their tendencies. At that point, what was most important to her was my wellbeing. With her swollen eyes she came to apologize for the actions of her husband. I was quiet for most of the time and overwhelmed by the situation. She explained everything but it seemed like he thought the American was to blame for every misunderstanding. Like Alicia, most empaths maintain or recover their strength or energy by ensuring emotional closure. She needed to talk through things with me as she felt responsible for what had happened to me. The emotional capacity of empaths can only be improved by finding this kind of closure with their feelings. Alicia would have remained worried if she hadn't talked to me. She actually left her home to balance the energy and emotions between us. In other words, they maintain their emotional strength by embracing and stretching their tendencies rather than running from them, although it is also important to observe caution and ensure that the expressed compassion is always rational. In a nutshell, empaths would only remain in a bad state of mind, when they feel responsible for some negative outcome. Above all precautions, emotional closure should be prioritized.

What Oprah Winfrey teaches us about Empathy?

The excellence and success story of Oprah Winfrey puts her in a good position to talk about empathy. She struggled through her childhood and faced a lot of difficulty in trying to become a successful black woman. There were issues with her parents and also issues in her marriage. Despite all the negative circumstances, she still remains one of the most successful women in the world. Her story is even more thrilling because she started and championed the cause of rich black women in America. In an interview, she talks about the role empathy played in getting to where she is now.

The three lessons Oprah Winfrey teaches us about empathy:

- **Empathy results from resilience in Adversity:** "The struggle of my life created empathy. I could relate to pain, being abandoned or having people not to love me." Like a lot of individuals, Oprah was a victim of abuse, assaults and serious family crisis when growing up. It took so much resilience and deliberate effort to really overcome the mental stigma that these events had on her. Now that she is renowned and accomplished, it is only natural for her to identify and want to support people going through the same. She does this with several NGOs, giveaway conversations, and even charitable organizations. Oprah teaches us that her positive application of her negative past was instrumental to the global acceptance of her brand. So we can all apply empathy to our organizational and personal life.

- **Empathy primarily fosters relationships:** "Leadership is about empathy; it is about having the ability to relate to and connect with people for the purpose of inspiring and empowering their lives." In her talk show, she uses the "rapport-talk" style where she indulges the audience in the conversations. Audience's perspective and opinions form the core of the show. Their emotions dictate the direction of the topics, this empathetic style to a TV show fosters the bond and relationship between viewers, audience and the host. Leadership or followership requires a good level of relationship and a great way to ensure a good relationship is through empathy. It puts you in a better position to understand and tolerate others.

- **Authenticity and empathy is good for personal bonding:** "Let excellence be your brand, when you are excellent you become unforgettable. Doing the right thing will always bring the right thing to you." The reason why most celebrities feel most comfortable talking on her show is because of the connection they develop with her. She is able to relate to even their most embarrassing moments and gives a platform for celebrities to properly air their views. Her unbiased and empathetic standpoints make her personal brand very authentic. The fact that she goes the extra length to help others express themselves makes her a globally renowned brand. She has been able to do this for 25 years now because she is not different from her brand. She sticks to her truth and allows people have their opinions and the global connection naturally falls into place.

The Most Struggles Empaths Prone to and Their Effects in Society

The struggles of an empath

An empath is an anomaly to a lot of persons. Sometimes their nature can even be baffling to themselves. The unique and extensive perspective can cause empaths to struggle, especially in a very complex world like the one we live in. Uncontrolled sensitivity and emotionally unhealthy relationships are some of the basic factors that can make an empath struggle. The keen interest of empaths developed towards animals, plants or even places is usually in contrast to the understanding of others. At some point, I found her behavior extreme and vulnerable.

Here are some of the struggles that empaths are prone to:

- **Anxiety and depression:** These are common states that empaths find themselves in. Contrary to some opinions, it is not only as a result of their affiliation or interaction with the negative energy of others. Empaths get worried or depressed by unhealthy perceptions and negative feedbacks from others. Empaths easily attain the extreme levels of this state due to causative triggers. As earlier discussed, these triggers are the factors that make individuals become empaths. It could be temperament or unstable parenting etc. Empaths have a natural tendency to end up being anxious or depressed. Alicia was so worried about my emotional health that she left her home for a conversation with me. She needed to do this to be at peace with her nature. Environmental or plant empaths also get anxious or depressed when trees are being cut down or when plants in general are not cared for. This applies to the other types of empaths who attain this state when their peculiar passions are disregarded. Most of the time, they are handicapped when nothing that can be done about them.

- **Emotion narcissism and energy drain:** Empaths are very intuitive. They use even the most subtle emotions and social cues to determine truth or lies. This easily sounds like a great ability for empaths. But despite this ability, they are still vulnerable to people that I call emotional narcissists. They take advantage of the compassionate nature of empaths as they always want to draw empaths into their situations. Their emotional needs are usually deep and thorough, requiring so much energy from the empaths. Naturally, empaths tend to connect with these narcissists and find it difficult to retrench this emotional involvement. Untrained empaths struggle with such people a lot as they find it very difficult to disconnect. The consistent pattern of negative incidences around me made it more difficult for Alicia to associate with me. This narcissism can also be juxtaposed to an ill pet that is surely going to die. The empathetic owner knows the pet will die but will still take all the available chances to save the pet's life. With all the energy and resources expended, the pet dies and the empath remains depressed and drained.

- **Unintentional, excessive, and overwhelming emotions:** Empaths often sense and receive emotions from others. This can be overwhelming in crowded environments where emotions are coming in all directions. The several emotions can be confusing and end up being mixed with theirs. With the inability to differentiate their emotions from the ones absorbed, this is obviously a struggle. This is a strong struggle because if all the emotions are taut, the connections and emotional interaction of empaths cannot be effective. This emotional struggle is also often faced by animal empaths. Some animal empaths go as far as taking in sick and homeless animals. And when the animal has recovered, they find it hard to let go of the animals. They develop a quickened connection with the animals.

- **Selflessness***:* Most of an empath's focus is on others. They make every effort to resolve the emotional baggage of others. This is often done to a fault as their own emotions are neglected. After Miguel left my house, he went back home and started assaulting his wife. Alicia knew the outcome of not giving Miguel what he wanted yet she didn't. Her welfare was never the concern. She got assaulted for it and am sure when another opportunity arises, she will do the same. If that isn't selflessness, then nothing is.

- **Flexible boundaries:** Some empaths actually establish boundaries to protect themselves, but they are often not observed. Empaths generally have the inability to say "no" or disappoint others. They would rather shift the boundaries or their emotional capacity to accommodate the needs of others. Their thin and flexible boundaries leave them defenseless as they almost allow anything and everything. This encroachment has a huge probability of leaving empaths drained and irritated. But if they say no, they end up feeling guilty and depressed. It is a very confusing struggle that can only be overcome by proper training. After Alicia dragged her daughter out of the class, she hissed at me indicating a form of regret or irritation. Yet she still came back to plead for me when the bandits wanted my life. After the bandits left, she hissed like she was largely angry and irritated by the incidence. One would think she would never associate with me. But when she got bruised for holding back my identity, she still came knocking on my door. She was more concerned about my wellbeing. She seemed to create boundaries and then end up not observing them or shifting the boundaries.

The effect of empaths in society

Society can basically be divided into individualistic and communal society. An individualistic society is one in which individual achievements and accomplishments are sought after. Nobody wants to do anything for others. In the case of communal society, priority is placed on community goals and objectives. Personal accomplishments are made secondary. The effect of the various types of empaths would be discussed in relation to the direction of their influence. Do they make society more individualistic or more communal? The influence of their tendencies and traits on themselves is an important factor in evaluating their effect on society.

- ***Emotional empaths have the ability to know the true emotions of others without even asking.*** They see through the behaviors, reservations or any other front that people often put up to hide their emotions. This discerning ability can go a long way in rectifying tendencies like suicide and depression. A lot of suicides would be averted if only there was someone to help carry their burden and rationalize their thoughts. Nobody actually wants to die but sometimes such people just feel so depressed and worthless at that moment. These thoughts might not be true, and it would only take a mature conversation to make such people disregard the thoughts. The challenge is usually how to identify these people that have suicidal tendencies. It takes highly sensitive people like emotional empaths to discover these thoughts. Emotional empaths definitely play a very important role in the social ecosystem. Also, there are a lot of people who nurse grievous ailments without having knowledge of them.

- ***Animals are a huge part of nature.*** They play diverse roles in maintaining our eco-system. Unlike humans, animals' feelings are extremely difficult to understand. To help animals, the first step is identifying and understanding them. Veterinarians are usually animal empaths as they are able to connect the behavior of animals to ailments. This type of empath helps to better society by improving the wellbeing of the animals.

- ***Plant empaths try to improve the society by advocating for the proper handling of plants.*** Plants and trees have good influence on the environment and its ambiance. This type of empath might not really be empathic because of the benefits of the good state of the plants. A lot of them just have a natural connection with them. The effective function of a plant empath can go a long way in developing society and the ecosystem at large. More breathable air to the increased greenery are some of the benefits that comes with plants and trees.

- ***Physical empaths are so connected with the pain and predicaments of others that they can feel it.*** A lot of this type of empaths end up as doctors or nurses who will sometimes go out of their way to give medical care. These are the types of doctors who will go as far as helping poor patients from their own pockets. These characteristics or empathetic expressions are another form of love. With so much evil and crime, love is direly needed to create the required balance and peace in society. The other types of empaths like the geomantic and intuitive empaths also help to better society with focus on particular subjects.

The effect of society on empaths and their self esteem

The effect of society can be seen in several ways. Firstly, society realizes the important role that empaths play. In a way, there is a great emotional demand for them. Society easily takes advantage of them due to their selfless nature. Even in marriages, empaths have to carry all the emotional baggage of the family members and partners. The relevance and the demand for emotional empaths like therapists is gradually on the rise. The effect of society is different for the various types of empaths. Intuitive empaths are usually considered creepy and encroaching. Since they have intuitive knowledge of things about to happen, people consider them as weird. This is even more so when what they foretell is negative. The geomantic empath usually has implicit expressions. Their connection or irritation by geographic location and places occur internally and influence their mood but naturally does not interact with society. A lot of the geomantic empaths end up as tourists, who are constantly seeking new places that they can connect with. The serenity of the environment and the balance of nature is often offset by human activities. Some are legal and others are illegal. A lot of this balance and serenity are maintained by plants and animals. The passionate advocacy by plants and animal empaths often leave them at loggerheads with the majority of society whose activities are often unhealthy to nature in general. Society wants to be more commercial. It wants more buildings to replace the trees and the farms. Society wants animals to roam the streets un-catered for. Society shows an unhelpful dislike for some types of empaths while too much is expected from the others.

Self-esteem basically means being confident in yourself. Empaths generally struggle with confidence as a result of the absorption of other's negative emotions and the constant exposure to external energy. It is difficult to feel good about yourself when you are immersed in the energy fields of emotionally dampened people. The consistency of this emotional interaction can easily ground the self-esteem of empaths. Good self-esteem is often associated or derived from positive accomplishments and emotions. Their carriage and resolution and many emotional needs and wants leaves them very vulnerable and stressed. They are stressed about the situation of others and sometimes their inability to do anything about negative incidences or provide solutions. This results in lack of confidence and they tend to struggle with self-worth or self-esteem. When Miguel was assaulting Alicia for refusing to tell him my identity, she didn't respond or react to the violence. She simply left the house in tears. This is obviously a matured reaction and it is what a lot of empaths would do in her shoes. The point is, this kind of reaction or tendency might be as a result of lack of self-worth or self-confidence. If she really knew her worth, she wouldn't have allowed anybody to assault her without resisting it. She doesn't have to retaliate with violence but should not expect the assaults like she had deserved them. **I would very much appreciate your thoughts about my book, please let me know on the platform you bought from.**

The Uniqueness and Roles of Empaths in the Social Ecosystem

The uniqueness of empaths can only be defined with respect to others in the social ecosystem. The traits they possess don't actually start in the forms described in previous chapters. There is usually an evolution of these characteristics into empathic forms. Although the uniqueness can be glaring right from a young age, so much development and guidance goes into making a good empath.

The evolution of empath's sensitivity

Just as earlier highlighted, the evolution usually starts from birth. Some babies are just more receptive and reactive to surrounding conditions. I like to call this condition Sensory Processing Distinction. The methods of expression or out forms of their sensitivity do not remain the same as they grow. It is important to note that the direction or form of evolution is greatly influenced by parenting and upbringing in general. These traits and attributes can be guided and developed for positivity.

The first stage of the evolution is based on touch, noise and sight. At birth, the empathic ones are either hypersensitive or hyposensitive to touch. The hypersensitive ones are uncomfortable with touch and they tend to cry. The feeling of the warmth from another person's hand makes them ticklish and insecure. Most times, this tendency is cushioned by the mother as the child begins to feel comfortable with the mum's touch. Depending on the parent, the child can remain like that or the trait can be developed to a socially profitable level. Others are hyposensitive to touch; they always want to be carried around by anyone. They tend to depend on the people around them to work or to do anything. These babies tend to cry a lot when there is nobody around. Empaths right from a very young age are usually hypersensitive. They squint their eyes at very bright lights, they cry when they are in different environments than they are used to. They can also be uncomfortable with totally dark places as they enjoy dimly lit rooms. Parental influence is often limited as the sensitivity remains at that height through several stages of growth.

This next stage of evolution is based on allergies and behaviors. Just before the teenage years, they begin to discover the things that greatly irritate them. For some others, their parents are the ones who first cash in on their allergies and behaviors. A lot of empaths are allergic to certain types, colors or even textures of food. Sometimes it is even the smell of the food that turns them off. As a contrast they discover the smell that they are attracted to. Some children always want to go to the beach every vacation just because of the subtle smell of the ocean breeze. Some empaths don't like bathing because they hate the smell of soap. The list is exhaustive as new experiences, new allergies and passions are discovered. Empaths also exhibit sensory avoidant behaviors and sensitivity to negativity. The sensory avoidant behavior is expressed as fear of heights, easy loss of balance, fear of fast movements (ski, skating, and bicycles). They also avoid hugs and eye contact. These self-explanatory expressions are the ways in which empaths avoid their fears and insecurities. At this stage, they begin to develop sensitivity to negativity and violence. They begin to realize that they don't like violent or tragic films. They would rather stay glued to romantic and comedy films with non-violent and happy endings. At this stage, they also discover what they are good at or bad at. This next stage is based on a tripod of noise, inner-conflict and social avoidance. Most empaths are usually calm, and they get mentally energized and emotionally balanced by serene environments. They are irritated and overwhelmed by noise and loud experiences. A lot of empaths stop talking when they can't hear themselves as a result of noise. They are usually the ones that would exit the class when the noise gets too much. Empaths have a common desire for a peaceful world and existence. Their experiences are often contrasting to this desire. This results in internal turmoil or inner conflict. They struggle with their desires and the reality of how unachievable they are. At this age, empaths realize how different they are from others, but their nature won't let them challenge the status quo. As a result, they develop a tendency of social avoidance and they seek closure in personalized activities like meditation.

At the last stage, they are inevitably involved in some social activities. Some are married, others are now parents. The irritation as a result of their relationships in the social ecosystem creates difficulty in self-soothing. They have less time and less ease in calming themselves. They go through a lot of emotional roller coasters and still have to satisfy the emotional needs of their husband, wife, children and friends. At this point, a lot of outside help is needed. Close acquaintances should be able to ease the burden and create boundaries for them.

The absence of this outside help can lead to suicidal tendencies and attempts. This is because they feel unfit in the world and they can't stand their incapacity in changing the narrative.

The difference between empaths and Highly Sensitive People (HSP)

Empaths and HSPs share a lot of common traits like easy emotional stimulation, quiet time, sensitivity to light and noise and distaste for crowds. HSPs are basically introverted people but empaths can be both introverts and extroverts. Empaths are typically an extension of the characteristics of HSPs. Empaths are highly receptive to the emotions, energies and physical sensations of the environment and from other people. Empaths struggle with the absorbed emotions and find it hard to distinguish theirs from those of other people. Highly Sensitive People don't typically do this. They don't get tangled with others' emotions and energies. They can sense the feelings and thoughts but do not internalize them, hence their less appropriate response compared to empaths. It is important to note that one can be both an empath and an HSP. A lot of HSPs are also empaths. Like Alicia, a lot of people can be HSP and empath at the same time. She connected with my feelings and emotions with empathy. This makes her an HSP. But a lot of the time she also got tangled with emotions and circumstances. Alicia constantly went out of her way to ensure my physical and emotional survival. The spectrum is between Narcissists, HSPs and empaths.

Empath Vs Empathy

Empathy means identifying and sympathizing with the thoughts, feelings or emotions of another person. It is a trait that all humans are capable of. Most of us can imagine ourselves in another person's shoes although empathy can both be positive and negative. With empathy, we react in correlation to the projected emotions. These characteristics are innate and can be expressed by most humans except sociopaths.

It is a way of understanding other's experience from their frame of reference. In some literature, an empath is identified as someone who is empathetic. This is not totally correct because an empath is actually an extension of being empathetic. Empaths do not rely on external cues, by intuition or nature they connect with the emotions of others (even the hidden ones). Other types of empaths connect to the experiences of plants, animals etc. They do not just connect; they interact with the picked up emotions like they are theirs. Some are even symptomatic to the condition and pains of others. There are some empaths that would have to overcome their own allergies just to satisfy the emotional or physical needs of others. For example, an empath is allergic to goats and there is an infant goat that just lost his mother and the squeaking bleats indicate that the goat is lost. The emotions of the goat might rekindle a past experience of being lost. Such interaction can make the empaths take in the goat and offer to provide appropriate care. This is in spite of the allergy and shows the extent to which an empath will go to help.

Here are the key differences:

- **External trigger:** For the feeling of empathy, an external trigger or a direct cue and interaction is required. On the other hand, an empath does not require a direct interaction. Empaths can feel the emotions without even knowing the person. As explained in the several scientific theories talked about earlier, they are subconsciously receptive to all the emotions around them. Like the experiences of a geomantic empath on the beach. The feeling of the legs on the sharp sand, the ocean breeze on their skin or the sight of the moving ocean tides. The reception of these combined emotions can be overwhelming and triggering. The average empath is easily triggered because of the ability to link incidences with past experiences. This is unlike an empathetic that requires direct contact (physical or emotion) before other emotions can be understood or connected to. The intuitive empaths connect experiences with emotions and are able to discern thoughts and connect with imminent incidences.

- **Healing:** Empathetic people can relate to other people's struggles and they tend to sympathize with such. Empaths connect and interact with the emotions of others so well that they can gradually walk them out of the negative emotions. They own the emotions but still maintain a healthy mental state to react, advise and respond appropriately. Their comprehensive understanding of the feelings, emotions and thoughts of others ensures their effective healing. This healing is not just emotional but can also be very physical as empaths are very caring. In truth, I felt better after the conversation with Alicia. It was easy for her to walk through the emotions while she attended to my wounds. I believe the effectiveness was from the combination of the makeup of their caring nature.

- **Accuracy of the connection:** The empath's help is even more relevant because they have the ability to determine the truth. They go in deep on the feelings, emotions and thoughts. This enables them to realize the suppressed or hidden emotions. Empath's interactions are often unintentional, so it is not influenced by unconcerned agendas. From the electromagnetic theory, even the other person can't hide the true emotions or thoughts while in the electromagnetic region of an empath. A trained animal empath can accurately discern what is wrong with a pet. This is unlike the owner who is just empathetic but does not have the ability to interpret or relate the behaviors to ailments or illnesses.

Why does the difference matter?

The differentiation of these two personalities matter because the two are actually not the same. In effect, they require different treatments and they have different motives. **Here are some of the reasons why it is necessary to differentiate between the two:**

- ***A lot of empaths need training to learn how to manage their abilities without depending on them.*** If the two are not differentiated and isolated from each other, empathetic people may end up getting trained for nothing. And an empath might think, training is not needed. This is important because a high percentage of empaths resort to addictions because of the overwhelming emotions. Empathy is a very good characteristic in humans and needs no form of training, but empaths need to be protected from themselves. Or at least they need to protect themselves.

- ***Labeling personalities differently indicates a more detailed understanding of their different characteristics.*** This gives a clearer relevance of each position in relation to others. If empaths and empathetic ones are identified and recognized under one umbrella, their different nature wouldn't be captured. If empath's tendencies are not well identified, their effectiveness will be greatly impeded. It might actually lead to self-conflict, because empaths would be considered as just any empathetic person, but it doesn't stop their tendencies. How will they feel if everyone considers them as empathetic if their sensitivity and emotional interaction is at a different level?

What empaths need to know in order to maintain their levels of empathy?

This is not about how empaths should protect themselves but how empaths can be more effective and accurate in connecting, absorbing, and interacting with the emotions of others. These tips describe how empaths can harness their tendencies for emotional resolution. They also ensure that the empaths are not totally overwhelmed while being natural. **Here are some of the methods to achieve this:**

- **Grounding and earthing:** This involves connecting with the earth's energy by grounding yourself. Nature plays a major role in the lives of empaths. Contact with special earthily bodies like lying on the beach, staring at the sky at night or your foot sole in water. All this helps to tap into the energy and emotions of nature. For a lot of people, this is a way of dealing with stress but it's actually a way of laying your emotional and energy demand on nature, making the earth your source of strength and the object of your conversation. In this process, the freer, the more the connection. These techniques actually work for most empaths as their passions come from being in tune with nature. The absorbed emotions by emotional empaths have to be laid on someone or something. Fortunately, nature can accommodate a lot of this redundant energy and emotion.

- **Massage:** Massage is a way of getting out of your thoughts and emotions and placing focus on your body. This is a form of physical meditation as it puts the nerves and pores in a very relaxed state. A lot of breakthroughs have been recorded by foot massages and backrubs. It can result in having different perspectives or a different overview of how to approach the emotional demands of others. The relevance is in the distraction from your thoughts and emotions and staying in a physical pleasure.

- **Vocalization of needs and demands:** This is not to say empaths should also make others their empaths. They should just be expressive, and their personal emotions should be identified, differentiated, and inputted in addressing other's emotions. This can prevent the mix of absorbed emotions and energy. Alicia continued to struggle because she was not vocal about her needs and emotions to her husband. Not that she didn't want to, but her husband seemed narcissistic. After she was done attending to my wound, it seemed like she couldn't stop talking as she had so much to say. The expression of her emotions and needs built her confidence and strength. It was actually the only time that I found her in a good mood.

- **Study and observe yourself:** Empaths need to be sensitive to themselves. If their emotions and energy are personalized enough, they are able to confine and isolate them from the emotions of others. A major stressor for empaths is the emotional mix up and acquisition of other's negative energy. Empaths should also be vocal about their feelings about their partners and friends. These feelings should not be suppressed. A lot of empaths suppress them so much that they become difficult to express or identify. Observance of oneself is the first step to personal development.

- **Practice positive emotions:** Things might not be going smoothly as the absorbed emotions can be very exhaustive. An effective way to maintain a balance is practicing positive emotions like joy, celebration or even love. This practice might not be obvious, but it can be very effective. Some of these practices include throwing an impromptu party, going on a self-date, spending time with your kids. Derive excellence and celebration-worthiness from the smallest of achievements. It might be artificial but in the long run, the positive emotions flow naturally. It is a very effective practice of overcome negative energy.

Fields where the rare gifts of empaths are relevant

The unique and special traits of empaths require certain conditions for optimum utility. The parasitic relationship often involved in by empaths extends to the workplace. As earlier highlighted, in the wrong environment (including work), the relevance of empaths can become detrimental. **Here are 14 jobs where empaths can make appropriate use of their rare gift:**

- **Nurse**: The most important part of a nurse's job is caring for patients. This is almost a perfect job for empaths as they can easily connect with patients. Their natural tendency to care for others forces patients to open up. In the case of grievous ailments, empaths can become a support system for patients. It is important to note that there is a tendency for empaths to get attached to patients and in effect act unprofessionally. For example, if a patient who the empath has developed a bond with is unable to pay the bills, she might find it difficult to let such poor patients go without treatment. Also, on busy days, the diverse accidents that are brought into hospitals can be overwhelming and irritating to such a nurse. Empaths can be a nurse in companies, private houses or hospitals.

- **Psychologists:** Psychologists basically help people with mental health issues. They study mental states, social processes, and behaviors through their relationship with others and the environment. Mental health is just as serious as physical illness. According to the WHO around 20% of the world's children and adolescents have mental disorders or problems. The problems of having an unhealthy mental state is prevalent and seriously needs urgent attention and treatment. Empaths would do a great job at this because of their naturally caring, listening and understanding tendencies. Their understanding coupled with the connection with other's emotions provides them with the capacity to give proper advice. Psychologist can work in clinics, hospitals, rehabilitation facilities, health centers etc.

- **Writer:** Writing is basically a literary way of telling stories, narratives or even ideologies with words. Empaths are highly prone to powerful emotions that can lead to captivating stories and writing. This is only possible if the emotions are channeled properly. As a writer, empaths can become freelance writers, bloggers or even an author.

- **Veterinarian:** empaths are generally in tune with nature and they can communicate and interact with the emotions of the several elements in nature like animals, plants, places etc. Animal empaths have the capacity to discern the subtle gestures of animals and they understand and can relate with the animals. So empaths who are vets can easily diagnose and treat sick pets. Their interaction skills can also help with the pet owners.

- **Artist:** The experiences of empaths equip them with unique perspectives and they often conceive and express emotions in a distinct light. Art is obviously about perspective and expression; the unique and different works are often captivating and valuable. Their powerful emotions and superior energy field gives them the capacity to create unique work which can be expressed in artwork. Most of the renowned and great artworks are often influenced by negative experiences or bad emotions. Their soft spot for others and making society better increases the probability of creating relevant artwork.

- **Musician:** Similar to writers and artists, the strong emotions can be directed into good music. As a matter of fact, the music can also be therapeutic. "Confession" by Usher is one of the greatest albums of the 21st century and it was inspired by a heartbreak (negative emotions). If the emotions are put into a song, it will be highly relatable for a lot of people due to its origin.

- **Life coach:** empaths have an innate nature to help others. They get satisfied when problems are resolved. The interests of others are the priority. Being a life coach is a perfect job for empaths as they are accurately intuitive and can connect easily with emotions. Empaths are in a good position to help others achieve their goals.

- **Guidance counselor:** This is similar to a life-coach but this time, the help is provided to a child or a young adult by mentoring them. Students will be assisted to achieve academic stability and excellence. Students often fail academically as a result of a bad state of mind. Empaths can help meet the mental needs and wants of students. Also, at the age of young adults, their mindset is still malleable, and they can easily be influenced.

- **Teacher:** A teacher's job is not just academic; it also involves offering proper support and motivation. The teaching aspect might not come naturally but the latter is just as important, and empaths can execute this flawlessly.

- **Social worker:** A social worker primarily provides support for clients and individuals. This kind of job would be very suiting for empaths because of their nature and ability to influence the lives of people they get involved with. Empaths in social work should be cautious because there is a tendency to fail clients. Not all social work will have a happy ending, and this can take a deep toll on empaths. So, it is essential for an empath to develop self-care habits and the ability to withstand the inevitable disappointments.

- **NGO workers:** Non Profit Organizations are focused on particular social objectives. The nature of such organizations requires workers who are not in it for the money but for the emotional and social accomplishment. The required level of dedication and compassion needed by the social workers is easily achieved by empaths.

- **Lawyer:** Empaths can help so many lives as an attorney. It sounds like an occupation that doesn't fit an empath because of the hard mindset that people had developed of lawyers. Empaths can represent domestic violence victims, non-profit organizations, or free legal counsel to charities. They should be careful not to handle more intense legal disciplines like trials. Their connection with their clients would ensure that they would go the extra mile to defend their clients.

- **Self-employed:** Self-employment is the best position for an empath to be in. They get to use their talents without stringent schedules or uncomfortable rules or even stress from the fellow workers and the work environment. Empaths can easily thrive in self-employment as they have so much control over the business. This doesn't reduce their empathetic tendency in any way, but the connection and emotional interaction will be at a comfortable pace.

The Needs of an Empath

The roles empaths play in society often leave their desires unattended to. They are so involved in the lives of others that they can forget their needs or confuse theirs with the needs of others. Empathetic relationships can easily be parasitic as so much is demanded from them. This chapter discusses the needs of an empath and what they should get in return. It is obvious that Alicia wanted the academic excellence of her daughter. She also wanted to achieve this without going against the tenets of her husband. After her husband had threatened me, she needed to make sure that I was okay. From the previous chapters, it is obvious that the needs of an empath aren't particularly substantial. They basically just want to satisfy others and sometimes themselves however difficult this may be.

What do empaths want in return?

- **Emotional satisfaction:** Empaths get involved in other people's situations not just because they can't resist it but also because of the fact that they want to solve the problem. They have an addictive desire to resolve negative emotional patterns and help others out of their bad feelings. Empaths are very happy when their interactions and connection lead to breakthroughs. They might end up being stressed but the breakthroughs are another enthusiastic incentive to want to do more. I personally think that her success in preventing the bandit from killing me was a big incentive for her to stay connected or involved. She hissed and remained disgusted after the bandits left but there was a definite satisfaction.

- **A better world:** Empaths want a society where people are not emotionally or mentally stressed. They desire a world free of so much negativity. Empaths want to be part of changing the narrative and that is why they always want to help. In a better world, they wouldn't always have to carry the emotional load of people around. Environmental or geomantic empaths need the environment to be in a very good state. They want the oceans and other water bodies to be free of plastic and toxic wastes. The plant empaths need more attention to be paid to the trees and agriculture. There are some extreme plant empaths who migrate from urban areas into tents in the woods. They enjoy the ambience of cooking with firewood and the smell of the wet grasses. In general, empaths want a better and healthier society that is free from negativity. Obviously, this is almost impossibility and that fact creates a lot of pressure and stress on the empaths.

What empaths should get in return?

- **Positive feedback:** Most empaths are just as sensitive to words and opinions. They read a lot into external opinions about them. As a matter of fact, a lot of empaths won't say "no" because they don't want others to think of them as unhelpful. There is an inborn tendency to get sad when others talk badly about them. A lot of these empaths want to hear what people think about them. Positive feedback is one thing that revitalizes their empathy. I am sure when Alicia realized that her husband came to fight me, she was bothered about the opinion that I must have developed of her. She felt she was the cause of the negative event and she actually took all the blame away from her husband. In our conversation, not once did she talk ill of her husband. She was just gushing apologies and trying to make me feel better in the midst of the negativity. Her emotional satisfaction also came when she realized I wasn't angry with her but with Miguel.

- **Appreciation:** Everybody likes to be appreciated and empaths are no exception. They want people to be as sensitive to their efforts and their emotional help. This can come from their partners, friends or even children. Because of the nature of their sensitivity, the appreciation can be a small gift or a friendly outing. They strongly appreciate even the smallest form of gestures. One of the reasons why Miguel actually got angry was the unconscious joyful expression on her face while she read my letter. The appreciation seemed like what she wanted. Empaths crave appreciation and it is often because they don't get enough of it from people around them. At the end of the conversation, she really gushed about the letter.

- **Better outcome:** The bad experiences of empaths in the past are easily connected to the present. Due to their highly sensitive nature, they can easily link a particular incidence with another in the past that created the same emotional effect. This creates the tendency for them to react personally to the situations of others. When Alicia heard the gunshot and the voice of the Mexican bandits coming up the stairs, she could have acted on the present emotion, which was fear. She didn't, she probably connected it with a previous incidence that provided her with fear. She might not have liked the way the past incidence ended, and she wanted to do better this time. Putting her life on the line for me might not be very rational but she didn't want to go through the negative emotions of being unable to do anything about such a situation.

Empaths and Addictions

When the absorbed emotions become too exhaustive for empaths, they often resort to mental distraction. Their heightened sensitivity gives them the capacity to hide their feelings, thoughts and emotions effectively. As a result, most people do not realize their negative state of mind. The distractions they resort to are often deep addictions. Empaths can achieve change in state of mind depending on the surrounding conditions like sound, light, noise. Picking up on the energy of everything around you (negative and positive) will naturally result in an emotional roller coaster. Addiction will always be a realistic alternative when the empaths do not have a good support system. Alicia can only take so much with the type of man she is married to. She is also a victim of the environment as the neighborhood is predominated by narcissistic Mexicans.

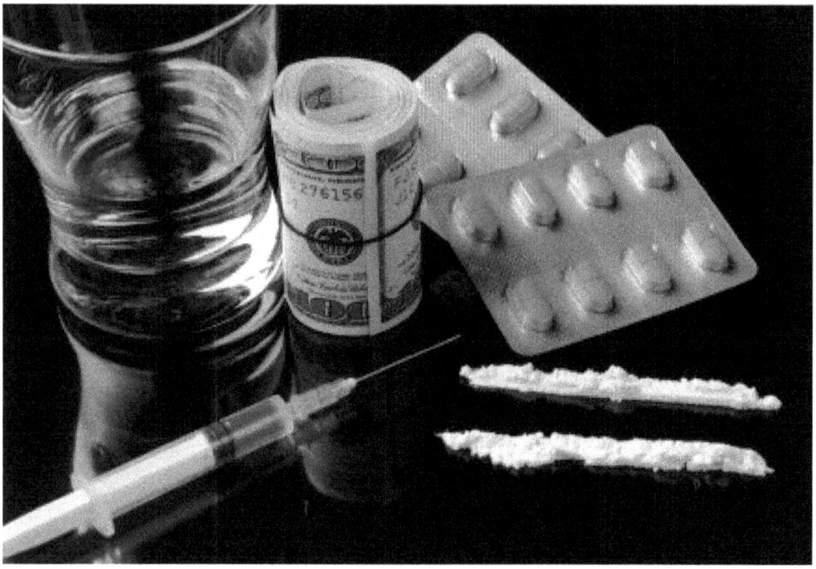

Common addictions:

- **Drugs and alcohol:** Empaths turn to drugs and alcohol to ease their empathic edginess. They drink alcohol to subdue their sensitivity and to make them less aware of the environment. The prescription sedatives, marijuana or spirits temporarily protect them from the insecurity in the world. Like every other form of addiction, it becomes counter-effective when the influence becomes latent. They remain the way they were or less. Unfortunately, some of these addictions become impossible to stop or live without at the expense of their health. According to Addiction Centre, about 20% of Americans who are depressed or have anxiety issues also have a substance abuse problem. Drug and alcohol addictions cost the US economy over $600 billion annually. These facts confirm the reality of this addiction being a viable option during depression. This easily results in apathy and social withdrawal.

- **Focus on the negative emotions:** I know a lot of empaths who seek succor in their negative emotions. They reach to their energetic fields and try to redirect and reconstruct the stressors and bad feelings. The good thing about this addiction is that it creates resistance to that particular thought or emotion. I am sure Alicia remained agitated when she wasn't sure what her husband had done to me. She wouldn't have been stable or satisfied until she had worked out her emotions with me. This suggests her focus on the negative emotion or the situation around me. It is actually this addiction that lead to emotional resolution.

- **Solitude:** In this addiction, empaths isolate themselves from everyone and everything. They ensure quality time with themselves and try to draw energy from their alternative universe. This helps them build a better perspective of their feelings and thoughts. Empaths are sometimes prone to avoiding their tendencies and focusing on themselves. I don't find this very effective as most empaths spend too much time on their negative emotions and thoughts in solitude. This is different from focusing on negative emotions as solutions are sought after. In solitude, the emotions and their resolution are avoided and cannot strengthen their mental state. Proper Solitude represents time spent alone but it actually docs not mean loneliness. Statistics have it that more than 60% of lonely people are married. This suggests that a person might not be alone but yet lonely. There might be people around, but you feel lonely due to the disconnection. Solitude can help empaths know more about themselves and improve their psychological well-being.

• **Exercise***:* Science has revealed a great correlation between the physical and emotions. A physical workout will help to properly channel feelings and thoughts; it also builds the mental capacity of empaths. This is like one of the most positive addictions. Exercises might take a lot of your time and get you sweating but it provides a lot of mental stamina and stress relief as a consequence. Exercises generally increase the heart rate, which eventually results in greater emotional strength. The truth is that exercise is a solution to a lot of disorders and negative conditions.

• **Herbs:** Some empaths seek to manage their anxiety and emotional depression with native herbs rather than a doctor's prescription. The use of alternative medicine in combatting emotional issues is gradually growing globally. It is important to note that a lot of the herbs do not have scientific backing. Proper regulations are not provided for these herbs unlike foods and drugs. Some of the widely used herbs used by empaths globally include St. John's wort, Ginseng, Chamomile, and Lavender etc. In a nutshell, herbal supplements are not an adequate substitute for traditional medicine. The herbs have a potential to cause serious side effects, they can also interact with other drugs due to their chemical make-up. To be on the safe side, empaths should consult a doctor before ingestion of any kind of drugs or herbs.

• **Food:** Empaths can raise their vibrations by ingesting organic foods. These highly vibrational foods can help boost the mood and their strength. The strength is required to overcome the emotional highs and lows. A large body of proof (although not direct evidence) now shows the correlation between food and mental health. A healthy diet can be very influential on the state of mind. Unfortunately, empaths often indulge in unhealthy diets while experiencing anxiety or when they are in a negative state of mind. Some empaths focus on junk food and just try to distract themselves, but this is very unhealthy both physically and mentally.

- **Sexual activities:** For a lot of people, orgasm is a heightened way of calming down. They distract themselves with the pleasure of their sexual desires. Some masturbate while others indulge in even more extreme sexual activities. This is one of the addictions that often make the feelings and self-thought worse than before, when it is done wrong or against one's beliefs. Nonetheless, there are several physical and mental benefits associated with orgasm. A spiritual empath can often feel less self-worth after immoral sexual activities like masturbation and fornication.

- **Gambling:** The unpredictability and the high stakes involved in gambling can easily get empaths engrossed. The possibility of a loss, the thrill of winning can temporarily cover the negative emotions and stressors. This is a very unhealthy addiction as empaths can also end up losing a lot thereby making their mental state worse than they were.

How empaths should deal with addictions

These addictions can be very hard to deal with especially by empaths. This is because of the consistent emotional roller coaster that they tend to experience. The lack of a good support system can also increase the tendency of addiction. Due to the numerous forms of addiction, empaths are likely to find a particular addiction that is effectively magnetic to them. Addictions are usually non-economical and irrational, which is why they shouldn't be held on to. **There are some action steps that can be used to deal with the addictions:**

- ***Identify your addictions***: The first step is to identify your addictions. There should be an evaluation of the addictions, questions should be raised and answered. How often is the addiction? Should you turn to another form of addiction or not? This identification will only be effective if the empath needs to be compassionate and easy with themselves. Self-denial is very prevalent amongst empaths, as they are scared of the way the world will perceive them if everyone knows about their addiction. Until the addictions are identified, recognized and owned, the solution is not easy. For example, Alicia had an addiction of focusing on negative emotions. She remained unsettled until she was sure the intuitions and emotions were balanced and positively executed. If Alicia did not know about this addiction, it couldn't be resolved. For her, she may just see it as her own caring nature

- ***Secondly, empaths need to realize that no external factor can overcome their addictions.*** The refuge or solution can only be evoked from the inside. Empaths just have to accept their tendencies and know how to control the emotions and energy. This is to ensure that they are not overwhelmed and do not resort to addiction. Empaths need to dig in deep to develop closure and handle their feelings. They can get succor from their support systems or professional psychologists. Even then, nothing can be achieved without empaths playing their part in self-worth and self-comfort. The process of overcoming addictions can be lifelong.

- ***Thirdly, empaths can indulge in psychotherapy; this is a very professional and effective way of addressing addictions.*** It is a diverse range of treatments that can resolve mental health issues, negative emotions or even disorders. It can help empaths understand themselves and ensures dominance of the positive emotions. Psychotherapy often yields a lot of breakthroughs in depression, self-esteem, and addictions. In psychotherapy, priority is placed on conversations and not medication. This is why it is often called "talking treatment." It is a two-way treatment and it often requires a good relationship between the client and the therapist that is built on trust. Psychotherapy comes in different forms and through different means for an amount of time dependent on the depth of the illness or disorder.

Conclusion

Empaths possess a very complex and delicate nature; this provides them with emotional capacity to care for others. All the various types have important roles to play in society often at the expense of their mental and physical health. This puts utmost priority on the observance of precautions and emotional boundaries. Empaths should surround themselves with like minds that can offer support when their negative tendencies are becoming difficult. The absence of these defeats every form of training that can be obtained. If Alicia had a very sensitive husband, she would have found it much easier to cope with the negative emotions. Her genuine nature always prompted the Mexican wife to her first intuition, which was compassion. Alicia would always connect or try to help people whose emotions she could relate to. I had to dissociate myself from her so that she didn't get hurt while trying to help me. This uncontrollable tendency expressed by empaths requires training to ensure mental and emotional safety. The traits of empaths evolve, and they need to be guided and developed. Parents have a huge role to play in how their personality turns out. Empaths play a very important role in our society and they should be encouraged and appreciated. This also puts an obligation on non-empaths to respect the boundaries of empaths and not overwhelm them with negative energy. Empaths often have the inability to say no and will take so many risks to help others. In the light of these emotions, they develop bad tendencies and addictions. A lot of empaths also resort to suicide when there is no proper support system. Some of these tendencies can easily be averted with conversation. **Here are some of the symptoms of suicidal tendencies:**

- Sadness and feeling of worthlessness
- Frustration and irritability
- Easy loss of interest
- Over sleeping
- Fatigue
- Concentration problem
- Changes in appetite

A lot of the time, some of these attributes can be suppressed but a combination of these often shows suicidal tendencies. The onus is on us all, both empaths and non-empaths to be sensitive to each other. Just a conversation can save a person's life.

Being an empath is a gift to this world which is full of egoism, greed, fear and massive pain and your sensitivity is an immense blessing. Imagine what world would be like if we were all sensitive and caring for each other.

Discover Your secret Spiritual Gift

Everyone possesses a spiritual gift ...
But most people never know it
Discover and unleash your spiritual gift today ...
When you complete this short quiz

Visit http://bit.ly/3aDUiNk

to find out your secret spiritual gift right away!

EMPATH WORKBOOK

Discover 50 Successful Tips To Boost Your Emotional, Physical and Spiritual Energy

Alison L. Alverson

Introduction

Do you remember a time when you felt so alive with all the wondrous energy of the universe? You could tap into the energy that ran through everything and you were intensely curious about all that was around you. You were tuned-in to your surroundings and you could feel your empathic and creative gifts awakening. You likely even had vibrant dreams and visions that came true. Your outer life felt magical and your inner life was nothing short of whimsical and enchanting. You were enamored with nature and, like a sponge, you soaked up all the information you could about subjects like science, animals, and art. You might even have expressed yourself through dance and music. It was a wonderful time when everything seemed possible.

But then, something happened as you began to share what you knew with those around you. People in your life were skeptical and maybe even frightened or angry. As they questioned your gifts, you began to hide them away. You even denied they existed, as you felt an increasing pressure to be "normal". Maybe you feel that this denial of who you really are is devastating and you can't keep doing it. You find that you're drained of energy by engaging with toxic people who continue to hurt you so deeply. You find yourself asking why the world has to be so harsh and you're wondering if your gifts are even real. You can't seem to find anyone who understands you and you might even wonder if this is all there is to life—misunderstanding and pain.

But perhaps now you feel your inner voice screaming out in desperation, "That's enough!" You finally realize that you just can't pretend anymore. Now, you sense you're experiencing an awakening and you're looking for answers and deeper meaning. As you look around, you start noticing what seem to be signs and synchronicities that are guiding you to a new path, a path where you can be yourself, where you don't have to change yourself to fit in. Still, you're not quite sure of the next step. You want a life where you can thrive in the warm glow of your unique gifts. You need to heal yourself and discover how to be healthy, happy, and connected.

In my first book, *Empath: An Extensive Guide for Developing Your Gift of Intuition to Thrive in Life*, I shared how you can recognize if you have this gift—and it is a gift—and how you can tap into it. I know exactly what you're going through because I've experienced this myself. That's why I decided to create this practical workbook to help empaths on this critical journey of self-discovery and, more importantly, self-acceptance.

With this workbook, you'll have a useful guide that will assist you with the difficulties and sensitivities that are so common for empathic people. It will be a great reference guide that will help you learn and grow as an empath and the helpful quizzes, journal prompts, and reflection exercises will give you practical advice on how to connect to your heart space, as you embark upon the all-important journey of self-discovery. You've already taken the first step—you're looking for help. You want to bring the magic back. Now it's time to take the next step—start using this book to grow into the healthy and happy empath you were always meant to be!

Keys to Understanding Your Empathic Ability

There is some vital information about empaths and energy that I want to talk about before we get into controlling the energy around you. I have found this very helpful for a better understanding of how to control the energy I sense around me. Let's begin by taking a short self-assessment quiz about the way you respond to the energies you sense around you. Mark the following statements true or false:

1. I frequently get overwhelmed or anxious. True False ? ?

2. Arguments or yelling make me physically ill. True False ? ?

3. I am drained by crowds and need alone time to revive myself. True False ? ?

4. I am overstimulated by noise, odors, or non-stop talkers. True False ? ?

5. I overeat to cope with stress. True False ? ?

6. I tend to socially isolate myself. True False ? ?

7. I need to replenish myself in nature. True False ? ?

8. I need a long time to recuperate after being with difficult people or energy vampires. True False ? ?

9. I feel better in small cities or the country than in large cities. True False ? ?

10. I prefer one-to-one interactions or small groups, rather than large gatherings. True False ? ?

If you answered true to 5 or more of these statements, then you're likely an empath, but even more, if you marked certain statements as true—1, 2, 4, 5, and 8 among them—you might be having difficulty managing the energy you sense so strongly. So, let's talk a little about energy.

What is energy?

Every living thing exudes energy. It is expressed by a subtle electromagnetic field that surrounds the organism. For an empath, this energy field is larger than most and its boundaries are not as well-defined as they are for other people. Therefore, it is important to understand how energy functions for the empath before we delve into how energy manifests.

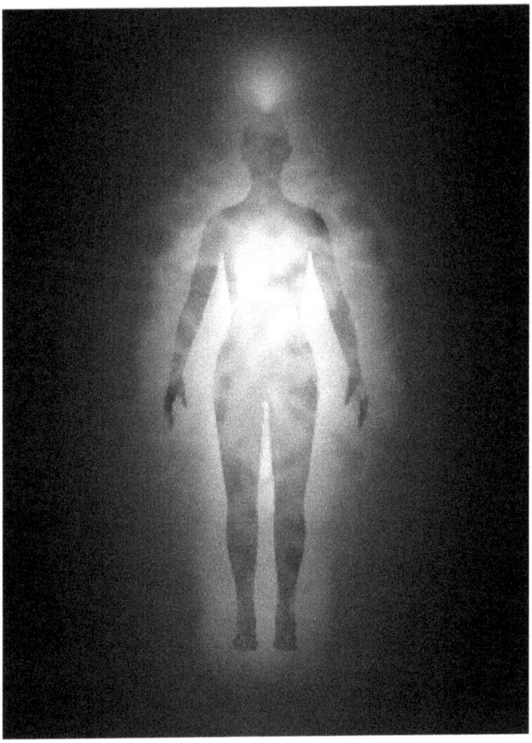

Energy is basically a form of fuel our bodies need to perform any activity. As you engage in activities, you spend the energy your body has stored and, therefore, you need to be re-energized at certain points. Now, many people can be re-energized by the mere act of engaging with other people, but most empaths tend toward introversion and, therefore, they feel drained as they engage with the people around them. Additionally, the energy field of an empath tends to overlap with literally everyone and everything around them. That makes energy management that much more important for the empath. They frequently need to get away from crowds and spend time alone, often in nature, in order to re-energize. That makes it very important for empaths to set healthy boundaries and to understand and respect their needs.

Journal Prompt: Take a moment at this juncture to write in your journal. If you don't have one, now is a good time to start one. Write down five things or situations that make you feel drained of energy. Next, write down five ways in which you are able to recharge your batteries. Do you notice anything about what drains you? Do you notice any patterns about how you are best able to recharge your batteries? Write down your thoughts.

How Sensitive are You?

Now that we've defined energy, let's talk a little more about how the empath manages that energy. Because the energetic field of an empath overlaps with other people and their surroundings, it can become very difficult to define your own energy versus that of other people. Additionally, because this energy carries with it information about emotions, thoughts, and intentions, it's very easy to be overwhelmed, confused, or even disturbed by this stimulation coming at you from all sides. To put it more simply, an empath is like a sponge, soaking up the energetic information all around them. Because empaths don't have the same kinds of filters and boundaries others have, they often absorb those energies they encounter in their surroundings.

Now, there is a spectrum of sensitivity. Not all empaths feel the energetic sensations around them at the same level. In order to manage the energetic fields you're able to sense, it can help to understand where you fall on the spectrum of sensitivity. To do that, check which of the following apply to you:

1. Do people describe you as naturally shy? Yes No ? ?
2. Are you easily influenced by others? Yes No ? ?
3. Do you find it difficult to say no? Yes No ? ?
4. Do people often approach you to ask for your help without provocation? Yes No ? ?
5. Do you often feel ignored or overlooked? Yes No ? ?
6. Do you often feel your sense of self or your purpose is confused? Yes No ? ?
7. Do you feel the emotions of others as if they are your own? Yes No ? ?
8. Are you a people pleaser? Yes No ? ?
9. Do you dislike being touched? Yes No ? ?
10. Do you sometimes find it difficult to identify your own feelings and desires? Yes No ? ?
11. Do you avoid crowds? Yes No ? ?
12. Do you often feel phantom aches or pains? Yes No ? ?
13. Do you need to be alone to recharge? Yes No ? ?
14. Do you feel overwhelmed in places, like hospitals, where there is an emotionally charged atmosphere? Yes No ? ?
15. Do you feel drained after being social? Yes No ? ?
16. Are you hypersensitive to the actions and/or opinions of Yes No

others? ? ?

17. Do you have problems setting a boundary with others? Yes No ? ?

18. Are you usually the giver and rarely the taker? Yes No ? ?

19. Do you frequently experience mood swings? Yes No ? ?

20. Do you accidentally or easily take on the moods and traits of other people when you are around them? Yes No ? ?

21. Do you avoid loud places or people? Yes No ? ?

22. Are you overly sensitive to violent or emotional media? Yes No ? ?

23. Do you keep your own problems to yourself? Yes No ? ?

24. Do you have a large capacity for understanding other people? Yes No ? ?

25. Do you feel driven to heal other people or help them solve their problems? Yes No ? ?

26. Are you highly intuitive? Yes No ? ?

27. Are you introverted? Yes No ? ?

28. Do you prefer to stay home as much as possible? Yes No ? ?

29. Do you find it easy to tell if someone is being dishonest? Yes No ? ?

30. Does it seem like you attract people who take advantage of you? Yes No ? ?

31. Do you feel like you have difficulty fitting in? Yes No ? ?

32. Do you frequently feel lonely?	Yes No ? ?
33. Do you prefer solitary activities?	Yes No ? ?
34. Do you dislike small talk or inauthentic interactions with others?	Yes No ? ?
35. Do you place an extreme value on your privacy?	Yes No ? ?

The more questions you answered in the affirmative, the higher on the sensitivity scale you are as an empath.

Journal Prompt: Write down in your journal how many questions you answered in the affirmative, as well as your thoughts about how sensitive you are based on this scale:

- **1 - 12**: Low sensitivity
- **12 - 24**: Medium sensitivity
- **Above 24**: High sensitivity

Which Kind of Empath are You?

Regardless of where you fall on the sensitivity scale, it can help to know what kind of empath you are so you will have a deeper understanding of the kinds of energy you're receiving, as well as the sources of that energy. Knowing this can help you with energy management. There are six types of empaths and I have included a short description of each:

1. **Emotional Empath**: This is one of the most common types and, if you are easily able to detect the emotions of those around you and, more importantly, if you feel these emotions as if they are your own, this is your type.
2. **Physical/Emotional Empath**: This type of empath picks up on the energy of other people's bodies. They might feel, for

example, a type of awareness in their own body in the area where the other person is having problems.

3. **Geomantic Empath**: This type of empath is finely tuned to the physical landscape. Often, these empaths feel inexplicably happy or uncomfortable in certain environments. It is because they are feeling a connection to the place. It may have to do with the history of the place—perhaps something tragic or joyful occurred there—or it might have to do with the sacred power of a place.
4. **Plant Empath**: This person intuitively senses what plants need. They have green thumbs and a gift for placing the right plant in the right place. They often choose to work in parks, gardens, or wild landscapes where their gifts go to good use.
5. **Animal Empath**: These empaths have a strong connection with animals and often devote their lives to caring for our animal friends. They have a gift for knowing what an animal needs and may also be able to telepathically communicate with animals.
6. **Intuitive Empath**: This person is easily able to pick up information about people by being around them. They can know immediately if someone is lying to them and they can provide all kinds of insight into the people around them.

Journal Prompt: Write in your journal the type of empath you feel you are and how that type of empathic ability presents challenges to your energy management. For example, if you are an animal empath, perhaps you feel intensely the pain of any kind of animal mistreatment. If you're a plant empath, you might feel the pain of deforestation on a physical level. Also, make a few notes about how you might be able to manage these challenges. Don't worry if you don't have any specific solutions right now, this book will help with that, but the goal is to get you thinking about your own situation and your own energy management strategy.

The Empath's Secret Weapons For Controlling Energy

Now that you have a good idea of your empathic type and level of sensitivity, let's look at how energy manifests itself for the empath.

Manifesting and Emotions

Because empaths have the ability to pick up on the emotions of other people or things in their environment, they can often feel bombarded by emotional energies. I know I did before I learned how to better manage incoming energy. With practice, you too can learn how to heal, project, work with, and amplify emotional energy, even negative emotional energy. Regardless of the type of empath you are, it is common for empaths to absorb the emotional energy to which they are exposed. This act, in and of itself, can make the people around you feel better. For example, people suffering from depression often feel better around an empath because they siphon off their negative energy. Well, that's great for the depressed person, but not so hot for the empath. This can create a situation where you are at the mercy of your own gift. But, with training, you can learn to take the emotional energy you're pulling from your surroundings and transform it, so it can be used to heal or manifest, as well as to project a happier emotional climate. Let's start with gaining control of your gift.

Tip #1—The Molten Empathy Technique: This technique can help you to free yourself of negative emotions and allow you to become accustomed to working with emotional energy. Use this technique whenever you feel an inexplicable negative emotion.

- **Breathe and go deep**: The first thing to do when you sense a negative emotion from your surroundings is to take a deep breath and look inside yourself to explore how that negativity is affecting your body. Negative emotions feel heavy, cloying, and/or dark, and it is that heaviness that is a clue. Locate where you feel it in your body and how it is holding you back.

- **Send the energy on its way**: The negative energy giving you that heavy feeling wants to go to the center of the earth, so take hold of it and send it on its way. At the center of the earth, it will be broken down to its purest form by the molten core. To send it on its way, visualize yourself pushing or draining or siphoning the energy down into the earth. See it flowing into the ground, past the roots and dirt, through the layers of fossils and rock, and into the liquid hot magma at the core of the earth. As you do, you will notice you feel lighter.

- **Pull in joy**: As you push out the negative emotional energy to the core of the earth, fill yourself up with the joy of blue skies, birds singing, and the celebration of life around you.

Practice this technique often, as it will help you to gain control over the way negative emotions affect you. In time, you'll be able to drain away negative energy before it is able to even touch you.

Journal Prompt: The next time you feel impacted by an inexplicable negative emotion, practice this technique, and describe your experience. As you write about it in your journal, answer the following questions:

- What kind of environment were you in when you felt the inexplicable negative emotion?

- What did you experience/feel?

- Could you identify an origin for the feeling?

- How did you feel as you drained the negative emotion into the center of the earth?

- How did you respond to filling yourself with joy?

- What did you feel after the incident was over?

Continue to write your experiences with this in your journal each new time you are affected by inexplicable negative emotions. Notice the patterns that emerge. What are the common environments in which you tend to experience these feelings? Are there people around and, if so, how many and what are they doing? Are there animals or plants around? Do these feelings tend to emerge in environments where there is a tragic or intense history? Identifying these patterns will help you understand your own experiences with greater clarity.

Tip #2—The Projective Empathy Technique: This technique is something you can use to help other people feel better when they're experiencing negative emotions. With this technique, you can remove the charge of the negative energy and help the person calm down. It can work to help a desperate person feel hope, a sad person feel joy, or an upset person feel peace. Since you're connected to them through your empathic ability, you can use this to reverse the direction of the emotional energy and project your own positive feelings into their heart. To do this, you need a reserve of positive emotions. These positive emotions are stored in your memory, so all you have to do is remember a time when you felt joyful or peaceful or calm. But, you need to have these memories at the ready and it can help to write them down.

Journal Prompt: Write down a time when you felt the following positive emotions:

- Joy
- Peace
- Calmness
- Happiness
- Hope

To project these positive emotions, you need to do more than simply remember them. You need to let yourself feel these feelings again. So, as you look at your list of memories, go back and relive those moments when you felt the flow of strong, positive emotions surging through your being. Practice feeling these emotions often. Not only will they help you be ready when you encounter someone who needs your help, they'll help you feel better too!

When you do encounter someone—or something—who needs your help, take the following steps:

1. Breathe deeply and choose the emotion you want to project;
2. In your mind, recall the memory that will evoke that emotion—relive the memory as if it were happening right now;
3. Fill your heart with the emotion from that memory, let it flood your being and feel your body bursting at the seams with this positive emotion;
4. When you sense the emotional energy beginning to overflow the boundaries of your body, send it to the person who needs your help—visualize it shooting straight into their heart. Feel the connection between your heart and theirs. This will cause their negative energy to transform into the positive energy you've projected into their heart.

Journal Prompt: Yep, you guessed it. It's time to write your experience in your journal. I know you might be skeptical of journaling, but it has helped me so much. The benefit of it is that it will help you to keep track of the progress you will make towards gaining more control over the energy you're picking up on from other people or things. You'll begin to see that you're better able to notice when you're receiving negative energy and you'll get better and faster at defusing that negativity.

Tip #3—Manifesting with empathy: You can use your empathy to help manifest your heart's desire into reality. There are numerous techniques that have been described to help you manifest the things you most desire. These include using visualization and petitioning the universe, but what is really at work here is the emotional energy behind the desire. Emotion is like a universal language and feelings contain a lot of energy. That's why they are crucial for manifesting. As an empath, you're intimately connected to the heart of the universe, so when you feel something, you feel it so strongly you can almost feel it into existence.

Whatever technique you want to use to describe your desire—whether it's visualization or another technique, the key to making it manifest will be to let yourself feel the emotions around what you want. What will it feel like if you have achieved the thing or situation you want to manifest? Let the feeling flood your body. Feel the joy or triumph as you've done it, you've manifested what you want! Project that feeling into the universe and you will attract what you need to manifest your dreams.

Journal Prompt: Write down something you want to manifest. Describe it as fully as you can. If it is a thing, what is made of, what color is it, what does it do, how will you use it? If it is a situation, what is needed, how will it help you, what will it look like in its final form? Describe what it is you want to manifest in as much detail as you can. Now, it's time for a little meditation.

Tip #4—Visualization Meditation and Energy: Visualization meditation can create a powerful energetic field. It's as if you transform your life in your mind and it allows you to fully sense the emotional energy inherent in doing so. Here's what you do:

- Sit in a comfortable position. You don't have to sit in the lotus position, but you also don't want to fall asleep, so sit up, but be comfortable.

- Close your eyes and begin by focusing on your breath. Feel it entering through your nose, going down into your chest as you expand both your belly and your chest. Feel it rising back up through your bronchial tubes and exiting through your mouth. Do this for five breaths.

- Now, visualize what you want to manifest. See yourself with the thing you desire or in the situation you desire. Imagine you have just achieved it. How are you feeling—triumphant, joyful, happy, excited? Let those feelings flood your body. Feel them in your heart. See yourself smiling and feel that excitement you had when you were a kid and just got exactly what you wanted for your birthday. Feel those emotions running through your entire body. Let yourself smile or giggle at the joy in your being. Visualize how having this will change your life.

- Express gratitude for this visualization practice and the happiness you have felt. Thank the universe for all it provides, for all you have right now, and allow the feelings of gratitude to infuse through your entire body. Feel those feelings of gratitude as they burst out of your body and enfold, first, those you love, then your community, then your city, state, country, and planet. Finally, send those feelings of gratitude out to the whole universe.

- Now, focus once again on your breath. Breathe deeply again for five breaths, and when you're ready, open your eyes.

The energy produced by this kind of visualization technique is a powerful tool for anyone, but that power is magnified when it is utilized by an empath.

Emotions and Health

I've been talking about how emotional energy can affect the empath, but let's take a deeper dive into how emotions and health are connected. This is something very important for the empath to understand because they are so strongly affected by emotional energy. To have good emotional health, it is necessary to first be aware of your thoughts, feelings, and behaviors, and how all of these are connected. It's also important to learn how to cope with stress because, let's face it, there will be difficult times in life. People who are able to cope with stress in a healthy way feel good about themselves and cultivate healthy relationships. But, even if you're someone who does have good emotional health, there are many changes in life that can disrupt that and lead to strong feelings of sadness or stress.

Even good changes that you want in your life can also cause stress. For example, you might be excited to move into a new house, but there's a lot of work that comes with moving and, on top of your already busy schedule, this can cause additional stress. Your body responds to this stress, regardless of whether it's good or bad. This is the mind/body connection that can lead to health problems if you don't understand how to manage your emotional energy.

Poor emotional health can result in numerous other health problems. The thing to understand about how your brain works is that it isn't able to distinguish between good or bad stress, it just sees stress and it activates the appropriate systems in the body to respond to that stress. What happens when you're stressed is that your brain activates what is called the sympathetic nervous system. This is the system that prepares you to either fight or flee—it's referred to as the fight or flight response. When this is activated, a series of changes occur in the body. Your heart rate increases as does your blood pressure, your eyes dilate, blood is shunted to the body's core, and a variety of corticosteroid hormones (adrenaline and cortisol, to name two) are released to give you the strength you need to either fight hard or run fast. Once the danger has passed, the parasympathetic nervous system is activated and it calms you down. When humans were living in the wild, where they could be eaten by a lion at any moment, these systems were necessary for survival. Sure, there are still times when your life might be in danger, but for the most part, in our modern world, these systems cause more problems than they solve.

The constant activation of your sympathetic nervous system can result in a number of health problems. It weakens your body's immune system, making you more likely to suffer from colds and other infections. You also are not as likely to take good care of yourself when feeling stressed. You might not exercise, you're less likely to eat well and you might abuse substances, like alcohol, tobacco, or other kinds of drugs. Stress can also manifest itself in a variety of symptoms, including back pain, chest pain, constipation or diarrhea, dry mouth, fatigue, headaches, high blood pressure, insomnia, heart palpitations (racing heart), sex problems, shortness of breath, stiff neck, lightheadedness, and an upset stomach, among others (familydoctor.org editorial staff, 2019).

Tips on How to Control Your Emotions

There are several ways to improve and maintain good emotional health. Let's look at a few of the best ways you can manage your emotions.

Tip #5—Awareness: The first thing you need to do to take control of your emotions is to be aware of them. You might think you are already aware of them, but you might just be aware of the initial emotion, which is often anger. To get to what's really bothering you, try this the next time you're triggered—stop and ask yourself why you're responding that way. For example, if you suddenly feel angry, stop, and ask yourself what is the underlying emotion. Often, it's that you feel hurt. So, ask yourself what is the core emotion that's underlying your first reaction. To figure this out, turn around and look at the "little you" that's feeling this emotion. Visualize yourself there in the corner or sitting in the chair and ask yourself, "Why are you angry?" What comes to your mind? What does that little you say? Is he or she really afraid rather than angry and, if so, why? Listen to that little you because he or she reflects your core self. This is what you have come to believe about yourself through time. It's the product of what happened to you during your formative years. During that time, it's common to bury certain feelings deep inside and to construct core beliefs from those early experiences. To process these emotions, you have to get at these core beliefs.

Tip #6—Process your feelings: When your "little you" tells you why he or she is angry or fearful or ashamed or sad, listen and give yourself the comfort that you might not have received when you were young. Be as sympathetic and kind to yourself as you would be to your best friend. This was hard for me at first, but it has helped me so much and it will help you too. You'll find you're able to heal a lot of early trauma using this method. This is a vital technique for the empath because it will help you genuinely distinguish whether this is really your own emotion versus an emotion coming from someone else. Even if it is an emotion from someone or something else, you still need to process it through your system. Try the molten empathy technique to send those negative emotions to the earth's core and replace them with positive emotions. For your own emotions, try writing about them in a journal (see the prompt below), or perhaps, talking about them with a friend will help.

Do what feel comfortable for you, but remember as you process these emotions, you deserve to feel happy and at peace, so whatever core beliefs you might have adopted about yourself, they simply reflect a time when you didn't have the coping strategies you do now. Now, you can respond in a more positive way and you can truly heal.

Journal Prompt: To work on processing your own emotions, write about them in your journal. What core beliefs do they reflect? Are these beliefs true? If they are true, how can you let them go—how will you be different? If they are not true, what is true about you? Be sure to describe the context for the adoption of that core belief. How old were you? What did you feel? How did people around you respond? Can you give yourself the empathy you would give your best friend? Can you send love and positive emotions into your own heart? And can you love even that little shadow self of yours, the part of you that you don't want to acknowledge? Can you bring your shadow self into the light of love? For example, if you despise selfishness, it's because a shadow part of you is very selfish. You might have felt and really been, selfish at one point in time—who isn't—and, after being shamed for it, shoved that little selfish part of yourself into a deep corner of your mind. Bring him or her out into the light and love that selfish you. He or she was only trying to look out for you, to make sure you got what you need. Appreciate him or her and welcome them into the whole of you. This is how you heal.

Tip #7—Set appropriate boundaries: As an empath, it is vital that you learn to set appropriate boundaries with the people in your life. Because of your gift, people will undoubtedly be drawn to you to process their own emotions. They will use you as a sounding board to process their divorce or layoff or other kind of loss. And, you likely want to help them, but you have to do so in a way that is healthy for you. This means boundaries. When they come to process their emotions with you, set a time limit and stick to it. It's not that you don't love them or want to help them, but you have to take care of your own emotional energy. You cannot be all things to all people and this is particularly true if you expose yourself to things that will negatively affect your health. So, let them know in a kind way that you can only spend so much time with them. And schedule in some time for yourself after their visit, so you can process the emotions you experienced through them.

You should also set boundaries for yourself regarding how much time you spend on social media and news sites. There's a lot of happiness as well as despair in the world and you often hear more about the sadness than the happiness on the news. This is also true with social media. It's very easy for the empath to get caught up in other people's stories because you feel emotions so strongly. This is why it's better to limit the time you spend taking in these stories. Finally, for any boundary you set, be sure to stick to it. It's easy to say, "Well, it's just this once—he's really sad", but remember if you compromise your own health, you won't be able to help anyone.

Journal Prompt: Write down five activities you engage in that can cause you to feel overwhelmed. Now, set a boundary for each of these activities. Be specific—for example, if you engage in social media, set a one hour boundary for reviewing social media sites once a day and specify the time for that activity, like from 9 AM to 10 AM. Institute these boundaries in the next week.

Tip #8—Learn to Let it Go: While it's great to really feel the happiness of joyful moments, it's also really hard to actually experience the sadness of tragic moments. As an empath you get both, and so you have to learn to separate yourself from the emotions of those around you. You can do this by practicing separation. You did not lose a loved one, break up with your partner, or get a bad diagnosis. You are not the one actually having the difficult emotions that those around you are experiencing. To separate yourself and let go, you can use a ritual, like the molten empathy ritual discussed earlier, or you can find a confidant for yourself—someone you can process your emotions with who can help you let go. Feel the emotions passing through you but *let them pass through*. Don't grab hold of them, they aren't yours. Try visualizing the emotions passing through you as you're experiencing them. See them moving through and exiting your body. Once they've passed, express gratitude for the richness of the experience.

Tip #9—Cymatics and binaural beats: Another useful tool for the empath is the use of cymatics and binaural beats to produce altered states of consciousness. Research (Raghu, 2018) has shown that visualized sound can affect your emotional state. Cymatics is defined as the study of wave phenomena, especially sound, and their visual representations. One area of this research is binaural beats. Binaural beats are auditory illusions that are created by two different pure-tone waves with frequencies lower than 1,500 Hz. There should also be less than a 40 Hz between the two beats and these two tones are presented to the listener dichotically—one in each ear (headphones are required). These beats have been researched for over 170 years and they can produce different effects on human consciousness. Every brain is different and so there is no exact answer to what you will experience, but some of the common physical effects are:

- Total relaxation of the entire body;
- Vivid visualizations, colors, and patterns;
- Separation of the conscious and subconscious mind;
- Relief from stress, anxiety, and tension;
- Feelings of sedation, or not feeling the body at all.

For the empath, the use of cymatics and binaural beats is something that can help them to rid their body of negative emotions and/or help them to promote positive emotions. Often, the beats are paired with carrier frequencies selected from nature and holograms for an optimal experience that creates a deeply meditative state of relaxation.

The tips I've discussed in this chapter are key to helping the empath manage the emotional energy they come into contact with on a daily basis. These techniques will help you to process the intense emotions coming from other people, animals, plants, and/or the physical environment. These techniques will also allow you to manage the emotions which genuinely belong to you and even to heal some of the early trauma you may have experienced. Think of them as your secret weapon toolkit and use them often.

Tips For Not Losing The Me In We—Relationships And The Empath

Because empaths are extremely sensitive to the emotional energies around them, maintaining healthy relationships can be a minefield. Perhaps the first step for the empath is to make sure you have enough control over the emotional energies to which you are exposed, so you are not constantly reacting to what you're perceiving. Practicing the techniques in the previous chapter will help you to do this, but it's also helpful to fully understand energy bonds and how they affect you as an empath.

Understanding Energy Bonds

An energy connection is simply a link or bond between two people, but particularly for empaths, once that link is established, it is not easy to break. Empaths feel these connections very intensely. The empathic mother may feel the pain of her child in every area of her body. She may know when her child is hurt, even if that child is grown and living far away. There are even high-level empaths who felt the pain of a loved one being attacked in exactly the same area of the body they are being hurt, literally blow for blow. These energetic connections between the empath and their loved ones are mostly passive energetic connections formed by strong emotional bonds, but it's also possible to establish an energetic link through the ritual sharing of power like a reiki attunement or some other ritual mixing of energies. These ritual bonds can allow the empath to know if the other person is okay or hurt or if they need help, but they won't always know what's going on specifically. They may know the other person is lying, for example, but not about what. This can be a problem for the empath in their relationships. They may know the person is upset, but not why they are upset. The energy can be just as strong if the person is upset about getting a traffic ticket, as if they are having doubts about their romantic relationship.

Sharing an empathic bond can be beautiful, but it can also make the other person feel uncomfortable. "You see too much" and "know too much" are common complaints from partners of empaths. Those with whom the empath share a ritual bond often find that they can make an energetic connection simply by thinking about the empath. Some empaths report feeling different energetic signatures from different bonds. For example, one empath reports that the energy from some of their bonds feels as though someone is cupping their face in his hands or hugging them. They report a sensation of heat—without burning—in their skin in the areas affected. It's not an uncomfortable feeling, but it's definitely noticeable. Other bonded people might appear in the empath's dreams as a means of connecting energetically. It is also possible to have a non-bonded connection as an empath. These are connections where the person might reveal themselves to you in a way that is not energetic in nature. Perhaps you see them as a translucent shadow, for example, but you don't feel anything in your body.

The energetic connections you make as an empath are called cords and you are creating cords with each interaction. It's also possible for energetic hooks to form through your interactions. Hooks occur when someone is trying to 'hook' into your energy. They might do this by, for example, saying hurtful things in order to hook into you and take away your power. They can put you down, make you feel unloved, or even try to shame you. Once hooked into your energy, they can feed off of it in a sort of energetic vampirism and this can even negatively affect your health. That's why it's important to remember that hooks can only be implanted if you allow them. You might, for example, be seeking validation from this type of person, or you might think you can save them, but if you respond to them for those motives, you are giving them permission to set the hook, and once set, they can keep coming back for more. How do you know if someone has their hook in you? Here's a few examples of how you might feel:

- You have a needy friend who contacts you daily to tell you about their issues. After speaking with them, you feel drained or 'headachy.'

- You have a coworker who finds fault with everything and, when you're around them, you feel frustrated and stressed.

- Your partner belittles you and blames you for everything, but even though you know the relationship is unhealthy, you feel powerless to move on.

Journal Prompt: Think about the people with whom you have strong energetic bonds. List them and identify examples of when you have felt your connection with them. What is your energetic connection with them like? Do you know when someone you love is in trouble? Do you feel it in your body? Do you see them as a non-bonded shadow figure? How does the energetic connection manifest itself? Once you have identified how the energetic connection manifests itself, write a few words about each person and how you feel after having an interaction with them. Do you feel energized, loved, worried, headachy, powerless? We'll come back to this list later, but let's talk a bit about how you can protect yourself from the negative effects of energetic bonds.

Tip #10—Protecting Yourself from Unhealthy Energetic Bonds: There are a few simple exercises you can perform to sever the energetic cords attached to you. These rituals do not cut cords of love and they don't remove the person from your life, they just cut unhealthy energy connections. I use these techniques frequently.

Exercise #1: Severing connections

- Sit in a comfortable, but alert position.

- Focus on your breathing and follow your breath through five inhalation/exhalation cycles.

- Envision a white light that emanates from your heart center and surrounds your entire body. Feel its protective glow.

- Envision the energy cords connecting you to the other people in your life attached to your solar plexus. See yourself using a sword to sever the cords of energy; watch as the severed cords pull away from you. Send them back to the person they belong to and now turn to the severed attachments at your solar plexus.

- Envision the white light closing and healing the wound of the severed energy cords.

- Express gratitude for the healing powers of your own energy, as well as the gift that allows you to make such intense connections.

- Focus on your breath once again for five cycles.

- When you're ready, open your eyes.

Exercise #2: Removing Hooks

- Sit in a comfortable, but alert position.

- Focus on your breath and follow it for five inhalation/exhalation cycles.

- Envision yourself bathed in white light emanating from your heart space and encircling your entire body.

- Now, visualize the energy hooks and notice how deeply embedded they are in your tissues. Gently remove them one by one. Each time you remove a hook, send it back to the person it came from.

- Repeat the following statement when releasing each hook, "I release this hook and return it to the person who sent it to me. I hereby revoke any permission I may have given, knowingly or unknowingly, that allowed this person to take my power or drain my energy". Now visualize the hook returning to its owner.

- Look again to the area of where the hook was embedded and visualize the white light bathing the area and healing the wound.

- When all hooks have been removed and the areas healed, focus once again on your breath for five cycles.

- When you're ready, open your eyes.

You can repeat these energy reclaiming exercises as many times as needed. You might need to do either exercise for cutting cords or removing hooks more than one time if the other person is someone you have known for a long time. And if you are still in contact with the person, the cords can grow back, so you'll have to cut them often, but don't be fearful of this process. It's simply part of the process you need to do to protect yourself. Another step you can take to protect yourself is to erect a shield.

Exercise #3: Erecting a Shield

Once you've cut cords and removed hooks, it's good to follow up by erecting an energy shield around yourself. You should do this shielding visualization at least once each day. Simply sit in a comfortable position and envision yourself surrounded by a shield that protects you from incoming energy. Your shield might be a white light or a mirror. A mirror works well since it reflects the energy back to the source, but you can envision your shield in any form you like. You can envision yourself safe from unhealthy energy as you sit inside your protective shield. Sit in the comfort and protection of this shield for at least five minutes each day.

Journal Prompt: Reflect on the experience of removing or severing unhealthy energy cords. How do you feel after reclaiming your own energy? Do you sense a renewed vitality? What are your concerns about the people whose energy cords you severed? What steps can you take to prevent people from once again implanting energy hooks in you? What does your shield look like? How does it feel to have this protective barrier? Allow yourself to explore any emotions you have about this process.

Once you have taken the necessary steps to remove unhealthy energy, remember to check in with your energy several times throughout the day. By removing unhealthy energy cords, you help to relieve the negative emotions they carry with them, like fear or anger. But, you should also be aware that by removing the hooks that these energy vampires have in you, you might provoke subconscious anger on their part. They might, for example, try to create drama to reconnect with you and get their hooks back in you. If that happens, just remain calm and reinforce your shield by visualizing it vibrating with strong, white light and reflecting their negativity back to them. When they see they will no longer be successful at getting their hooks into you, they'll move on.

You might be wondering how to identify these energy vampires in your life. Well, as we discussed, one way is to check in with how you feel after interacting with different people in your life. The energy vampires will leave you drained, headachy, or even feeling ill. But in addition to this, these are the people who create added drama in your life. They don't take responsibility for their actions, they act like martyrs, they try to make you feel guilty if you don't do what they want, and they tend to diminish your problems while playing up their own. They also try to always 'one-up' you and, if all else fails, they resort to bullying to get their way. In short, they use you for what you give them, but their friendship is a one-way street, where they always receive and you always give. These are energy vampires and, if it is possible, it is always best to avoid having them in your life. If you aren't able to get them out of your life altogether, you can protect yourself using these techniques. When they see they can't take advantage of you anymore, they'll likely move on. Whether they do or not, it's important for you to set appropriate boundaries that meet your needs in a relationship, so let's talk about that some more.

Tip #11—Setting appropriate relationship boundaries: I've already talked about setting boundaries in the context of managing your energy and the work you might do with people in your life around that. But, now we need to talk about setting relationship boundaries and maintaining them for your own good health. As an empath, the emotional connection you have with the people in your life is something you feel more intensely than other people. It's easy to get drawn into the drama in their lives and take it on for yourself. This is particularly true with intimate relationships. But, if you don't take care of yourself, you won't be able to help anyone else. So, how do you set boundaries? Let's start with understanding what it is you want.

1. **Name your limits**: Before you can set boundaries, you have to know what the limits are for each area of your life. The first step to setting boundaries is to identify them. What are your physical, emotional, mental, and spiritual limits? What can you tolerate and accept versus what makes you feel uncomfortable and stressed? In the space below, identify five limits you know you have.
2. **Tune into your feelings**: This is key to understanding your limits. Try rating your feelings on a scale of one to ten. Anything that rates a six and above is considered at the higher end. So, when you're having an interaction and you find yourself feeling uncomfortable, rate the level of discomfort and ask yourself what is it that is causing this level of discomfort? Is it what the person is saying or how they're

saying it? What is bothering you about the interaction? The feeling of discomfort signals that the other person has crossed a boundary, but you want to explore exactly why that boundary exists for you.

For example, you might have a fear that you're not a good enough spouse and, during an interaction with your partner, you might begin to feel resentment. It could be that what your partner is saying makes you feel guilty, like you're not doing a good enough job as that person's spouse. Now, once you've identified that's the problem with the interaction, you have to ask yourself a few tough questions. Do you feel what your partner is saying is correct? Is it true? If it is true, does it violate your own expectations for yourself or is it violating the expectations of your partner? If it is violating your own expectations, what can you do to improve the situation so that you live up to what you expect of you? If it is violating the expectations of your partner, but these are not your expectations or values, can you communicate that respectfully to your partner?

Let's take a closer look at this one, because it feeds into the other requirements for setting and maintaining healthy boundaries. Let's say, for example, your partner is upset because you're not spending enough time with them. The first thing to ask is what is the definition of enough time for you and for your partner? If your partner says, "I want you to spend every free moment with me", that's a high expectation on their part, but if they say, "I want a date night every week", that's something you can likely achieve. Once you have identified the expectation for each of you, now you have to realistically assess whether you can meet their needs. As an empath, you likely need a sufficient amount of time alone. Can you get that and fulfill the needs of your partner, as well? If your partner is asking for more than you can give, you have to be prepared to set a firm boundary and be direct in communicating that boundary to them. By opening clear lines of communication, you can understand your needs as well as those of your partner, you can respectfully reach compromises where possible, and you can also respectfully stand firm in your set boundaries, because you will know you are, in fact, a good spouse by exploring their concerns in a thoughtful manner. In the space below, name and rate your five most important needs in an intimate relationship. How much alone time do you need to recharge your batteries? How much time do you feel is important to spend together each day, week, month? What are the most important things you want to get out of a close relationship? Answer those questions and elaborate as needed—go to your journal if you need more space.

1. **Give yourself permission**: It's easy to feel guilty for having a need, particularly for the empath. We are taught in our culture to put our own needs aside in favor of others. What you have to realize, however, is that setting boundaries is not just a sign of a healthy relationship, it's also a sign of healthy self-respect. You deserve to feel comfortable and to live your life as you want to live it. Give yourself permission to set the boundaries you need to feel comfortable, happy, and peaceful in your own life. In the space below, write out five things you nccd in your life to feel comfortable, happy, and at peace. For each one of these things, write out a sentence beginning with, "I deserve..." For example, you might write, "I deserve time alone to recharge my battery so I will have energy to do the things I love to do".

2. **Directness**: Maintaining healthy boundaries requires directness. You must communicate clearly to anyone you are in a relationship with what you need in terms of space, time, and styles of communication. Whatever your need, you have to communicate it directly so that there is no misunderstanding. Directness does not mean be rude, rather, you can state your needs in a respectful way. For example, "I love you very much, but I need a lot of time alone. I need at least one hour each day after work to recharge my battery before we do anything together. Allowing me this time will mean I have more positive energy to put into our activities together. That's important to me, because I want you to enjoy being with me as much as I enjoy being with you". Now, practice being direct. In the space below, identify one person with whom you need to set a boundary. Clearly articulate your limit and what you need to improve the relationship. Then, write out a respectful and kind way to let that person know the boundary you are setting. State it directly, but respectfully—if you need more space, go to your journal.
3. **Make self-care a priority**: Particularly for empaths, the reality is that if you're unhappy, the other people in your life will be unhappy, as well. You not only have the ability to receive and feel their emotions, you have the ability to forcefully project your own emotions outward. That's why you have to make your own needs a priority. That doesn't mean you don't compromise in your close relationships, but it does mean that your priority must be with taking care of yourself. You need to be aware of and honor your feelings and needs. By taking care of yourself, you will ensure you have the energy to help your loved ones when they need you. You'll be a better friend, spouse, parent, and coworker if you ensure your needs are met. In the space below, list five ways you can improve on your self-

care and write out a plan for doing just that. For example, you might list practicing morning meditation and your plan for implementing that could begin with 15 minutes of meditation each morning.

By practicing these boundary setting exercises, you'll be better able to identify your needs and where you might need to set better boundaries in order to take good care of yourself. But, sometimes you engage in toxic relationships and this is an area of particular vulnerability for the empath.

The Empath and Toxic Relationships

If you practice good self-care and are aware of and responsive to your own needs, you'll likely avoid engaging in toxic relationships, but empaths are particularly susceptible to this, because they feel emotional energy so intensely. To identify if you're in a toxic relationship of any kind, ask yourself the following questions:

- How do I feel in the company of that person?
- Am I my authentic self when I'm around that person?
- How does it feel when I leave their company?
- Do they make me feel creative and inspired?
- Do they make me feel supported?

If your answers to these questions are negative—you don't feel positively when you're in their company, you're not authentic self, you feel much better when you leave their company, they don't inspire you to be better or act on your creative ideas, and you don't feel supported in their presence—this is likely a toxic relationship. It's a one-way street and you're always going against traffic. Because of their giving and sensitive nature, most empaths are engaged in at least one toxic relationship. They want to help others heal and they can see the good in everyone, but that means it is sometimes easy for other people to take advantage of their kind nature. So, how can you say goodbye when you're in a toxic relationship?

Because the empath is so sensitive to emotional energy, it's hard for them to let go suddenly. That's why it is often better to slowly retract using a process rather than simply cutting the cord at one time. The process starts with distancing yourself from the person. This can take two to three weeks to do effectively. Begin with small steps. For example, if you eat lunch together every day, then make it every other day. By slowly adjusting your time together, you both are able to establish new routines. Then, begin enjoying time with those people who fill you up with positive emotions. You will be feeling two sets of pain when you disengage from this toxic relationship and so you'll need strong emotional support. Call in the backup and make sure you take extra time for self-care. The last step is to formulate a plan for ending the relationship. Not every relationship will end in the same way. A coworker is different from a lover or a family member. Sometimes the relationship can't end entirely (as with a family member, for example), but you can set new and strict boundaries on when and how you interact. Whatever the plan is, make sure it is something you can carry out and remember that you must stick it out if you are going to truly take care of yourself. You are deserving of every good thing in your life and you have a right to take the necessary steps to ensure your happiness and peace of mind.

The Underestimated Challenges Empaths Face And How To Overcome Them

To maintain a high level of physical and mental energy, it is extremely important for the empath to take care of themselves. Because of their increased sensitivity, empaths often underestimate certain challenges that plague everyone, but impact the empath in a particularly severe manner. I know there were times in my life when I was guilty of underestimating these challenges and I had to make some changes to improve my energy flow. It cannot be understated that protecting and cultivating energy is important for the empath. So, let's look at some of the challenges that can compromise your energy as an empath and you can overcome them:

• **Physical and Mental Fatigue**: This is a huge problem for the empath who is so connected to everyone else's energy that they sometimes fail to recognize deficits in their own energy. That's why it is extremely important for the empath to get sufficient sleep and reduce stress. We talked about how the sympathetic nervous system is also known as the fight or flight nervous system. It gears you up for the fight or the flight, but in doing so, it secretes hormones like adrenaline and cortisol and these can negatively impact your health. Additionally, because your brain sees any kind of fear as requiring the activation of this system, even those non-life threatening fears like, "I'm afraid I'll lose my job" or "I'm afraid my car will break down", cause the activation of this system. This results in adrenal fatigue and can affect your sleep patterns, as well as your general sense of wellbeing. What can you do?

First, learn how to stimulate your parasympathetic nervous system—that's the one that calms you down. There are a number of scientifically proven ways to activate your vagus nerve, which is effectively the heart of the parasympathetic nervous system. These include meditation that uses chanting, deep breathing techniques that expand your belly as you inhale, massage therapy, and even singing in the shower. When the vagus nerve is activated, the parasympathetic nervous system activates hormonal responses that help calm you down and leave you with peaceful, good feelings.

Tip #12—Chanting meditation: Try this technique to utilize several ways at once to activate the vagus nerve and your parasympathetic nervous system. Do this meditative technique every morning and, when you are faced with a crisis, do an abbreviated version for just a few minutes to help keep you calm:

a. Sit in a comfortable, but alert position and close your eyes;
b. Focus on your breath—take deep breaths, inhaling the air and expanding both your belly and your chest as you do. Do this for 10 inhale/exhale breathing cycles.
c. Begin chanting 'Om'. Try extending the 'Om' sound so that you can feel your vocal cords vibrating. The vagus nerve innervates your vocal cords and doing this activates the nerve. Continue chanting for several minutes.
d. Visualize yourself in a peaceful place of your choosing. Let yourself feel the tranquility and the calmness of this place. Feel the calm energy entering your body, filling you up and charging your batteries.
e. Express gratitude for this time you've taken for yourself and let that feeling of gratitude infuse your entire body. Now, send it

out to the universe.

f. Focus again on your breath. Repeat 10 inhale/exhale cycles of breathing expanding into your belly. When you're ready, open your eyes.

If you're experiencing insomnia related to this physical and mental fatigue, try this meditation technique before bed in the evening. You can use an abbreviated version of deep breathing and visualizing your peaceful place when you find you're triggered during the day.

- **Physical Health**: When you get caught up in the emotional energies around you, it is easy to forget to take good care of your physical energy. We're talking about diet and exercise here, but let's look at a few specific tips for the empath.

Tip #13—Dietary choices: Because you're energetically attuned to other people, animals, plants, and the environment, you'll want to make choices that show respect and compassion for life as a whole. The best choices will nourish your body and your soul. When deciding what to eat, you might ask yourself the following questions:

a. Is this food produced in a healthy way that nourishes my body without introducing unwanted chemicals?
b. Is this food produced in a manner that is consistent with my values?
c. Am I providing my body with the necessary nutrients to keep it healthy?
d. Does the way I eat show respect and compassion for my health and my body?

If the answers to those questions cause you to feel bad in any way, you might want to consider making better choices. You'll also want to make choices that best nourish your body. You'll want to reduce your intake of refined sugar and starchy foods. Does that mean you can never eat these things? No, but everything in moderation is a good rule and, if you have specific health problems, you might need to eliminate certain additives, like salt if you have high blood pressure. This might seem like a huge ask, but the reality is when you reduce your intake of harmful foods, you'll start to feel so much better that you'll know it was worth the sacrifice and, eventually, it won't feel like a sacrifice at all.

Tip #14—Exercise: Exercise is extremely important for the empath because it is one way to release built up emotional energy. Of course, you have to choose an exercise regimen that is right for your level of fitness and any health challenges you have, but it's also important to choose an exercise program that resonates with your sensitivities. For example, dance routines can help to express and expel the emotional energy you've built up and they provide a way for you to express yourself artistically. So, think about what kind of movement resonates with you. Is it dancing or running or yoga? Any of these can be helpful for discharging that absorbed energy and—bonus—exercise, like yoga, also stimulates the vagus nerve and your parasympathetic nervous system. If you're just starting out, take it slow and build up in a healthy way.

- **Mental Health**: This is extremely important for the empath because of the absorbed energies they take on. You really have to take care of your mental health. I've discussed several strategies to employ to help you offload absorbed emotional energy and I've talked about the importance of setting boundaries. You should use these techniques regularly, but you also need to do things that you enjoy and that help to relax you.

Tip #15: Relaxing activities--This might include getting out into nature on a regular basis, planning some alone time, processing your emotions with a good friend, or creating real or imagined distance where needed. This could also include activities that allow you to express your artistic side.

Tip #16: Seek Professional Help if Needed—It's also important to note that there is no shame in getting professional help when you feel you can no longer effectively help yourself. A professional can lend an objective ear where a friend is biased on your behalf. Taking care of yourself is of paramount importance and, because of your sensitive nature, it is easy to suffer emotional angst. If you're going to help anyone else in your life, you must first help yourself.

These strategies will help you to overcome these often underestimated challenges that can forcefully impact an empath. By practicing good self-care, you'll find your own energy will soar.

The Mystical Way: The Empath And Spirituality

It's often easy to feel overwhelmed as an empath. I have felt this way myself and I know it can be easy to feel like this gift is a burden, but the reality is that becoming empathic is part of the process for spiritual awakening. Part of spiritual awakening involves a shift in consciousness that makes anyone more empathic and for those who are already an empath, that shift in consciousness can bring an increased sense of being overwhelmed. This is another reason it's important to understand how to manage those energetic sensations you're feeling. But, before I address this further, let's look at a few signs that indicate you are undergoing a powerful spiritual awakening:

- One big indicator of a spiritual awakening is that what you feel is something that is impossible to put into words. You feel different, but the feeling is so distinct that you can't explain it. It's as if the world was in black and white before and now it's in vivid color. It even has a new taste, but really what's changed is the eyes through which you're looking at the world. Suddenly, you see what's real and what's an illusion.

- You also see what has been negative in your life. You realize what represents the old you and you know that you don't want to do these negative or destructive things anymore. You're ready for something new and you want nothing but good for yourself and everyone else.

- You might also feel the need to seek out other people who are also experiencing their own awakening. Just like with anything else in your life, it helps to have people who get where you're coming from and that's just as true with a spiritual awakening. Many people who are currently in your life might not understand what you're going through and you might, therefore, find yourself seeking out those who will understand.

- You might also find that you now avoid anything superficial and people or things who are not authentic. When you plug into what is real, it's very hard to continue with those things that are distractions or superficial. You might find that you avoid people, places, and activities that don't express the authenticity you're now experiencing for yourself. It's easy to view this as antisocial, but it's simply a healthy sign that you are tuning in to the universal soul.

- You are also quite likely to feel a deep compassion for all entities. You'll be more highly attuned to both the joy and the suffering in the world and you'll experience these feelings very deeply. It can even cause depression if you don't know how to process what you're experiencing.

- You will also likely experience a need to make the world a better place and to have a positive impact on those around you. You might not know how to best accomplish this, but if you keep yourself open and grounded, the way will be revealed to you.

As you grapple with the immensity of a spiritual awakening, there are a number of things you can do to help you grow in this experience.

Let's examine a few techniques that can help you to grow into this new reality.

Tip #17—Journaling: I know I probably sound like a broken record, but expressing your feelings is one of the best ways to process your spiritual awakening, particularly for empaths. One of the things I have experienced is a feeling that I'm not doing my spiritual awakening correctly. I think that's a common feeling, particularly if you don't suddenly find yourself free from all negative emotions, floating on air like a saint. But, as I processed my experiences through journaling, I came to see that it's not about not feeling negative emotions, it's about feeling everything and then letting those feelings pass through you, while you stay grounded in the present moment.

Tip #18—Stay grounded: To say stay in the present moment seems easy, but it's more complicated than it seems. When the present moment is something mystical and joyful, it's easy to stay there, but when it's frustrating or frightening, well that's a horse of a different color. What I have to come to understand through my experience is that the point of being in the present moment is precisely to feel everything in that moment, to live it fully. So, how do you process it? You have to let the feelings flow through you without grabbing onto them and the story your ego wants to create around them. For example, if something frustrating is happening, your ego might start whispering in your ear, "You're not good enough. You need to get angry. You need to let them know who you are". But, that's just your ego trying to tell you a story and it wants you to believe that story. Once you recognize that and call it out, you get it out of the way so that you can let go of the feelings you're experiencing.

Tip #19—Sit with your feelings: You have to let go of any story your ego wants to tell you in order for the feelings you're experiencing to be able to flow through you. But, you also have to be willing to actually experience those feelings. That's hard when they're negative. To sit with these more difficult feelings, try getting someplace where you can express these feelings freely and simply let yourself feel them. Whether it involves anger or sadness, let them flow freely. As they do, notice how it feels in your body. Where do you experience the anger in your body? Where do you experience the sadness in your body? Let yourself cry or yell or curse. This is part of fully experiencing the richness of life in all of its emotional expressions. Once you sit with these feelings and notice their effect on you, you will also notice as they simply move on and you will feel better.

Tip #20—Understand core beliefs: This is another part of processing the intense feelings you're likely to experience with a spiritual awakening. Almost everyone accepts some negative core beliefs about themselves as they grow up and get beat up by life. When you're experiencing something like anger or shame, you want to get at the core belief behind your emotional reaction. This is an exercise we discussed before, but it's a very effective one. Turn around and see your little self-feeling angry or hurt or ashamed and ask him or her why they feel that way. Now, listen to the answer and then provide them with the comfort that little you should have received the moment the core belief was adopted. Let's take an example to explain this more.

Perhaps that little you did something you shouldn't have done—haven't we all? Maybe you got in trouble and maybe in a moment of frustration, a parent or guardian said something like, "How could you be so stupid?" At that point, that little you might well have adopted the core belief, "I am stupid". So, when you find yourself in another situation later in life where you're feeling ashamed, your little you might say, "I feel bad because I'm so stupid". Now is your chance to heal that old wound. Tell that little you, "I understand why you feel that way. Your mother asked how you could be so stupid and now you think that's true. But, you know what I know about you? I know you're a survivor and even though you sometimes make mistakes, that doesn't mean you're stupid. It means you're human and I love you, even when you do something wrong". That's the message you should have gotten, but everyone makes mistakes, including the parent or guardian who might have told you something like that. Being your own hero will help heal your old wound and bring the light of compassion to yourself and those who might have harmed you. By practicing this exercise, you'll find you can heal many of your old wounds.

Journal Prompt: Now, it's time for you to practice the exercise above. Think of a time when you felt angry or ashamed and take yourself through the process of understanding the core belief behind your feelings. What did you come to believe about yourself? Can you take yourself back to the moment where you formed your core belief and allow yourself to see the entire context of what occurred? Can you understand why you did the things you did? Even if now you think that what you did wasn't smart, can you understand why that younger you did the best he or she could in the moment? Can you have compassion for your younger self? Can you have compassion for any of the other people involved? Can you see their struggles? Let yourself feel any emotions that arise and notice what is the story attached to the emotion. Can you sit with these emotions and allow them to work their way out of your body? Let them flow and bless them on their way. Write about this experience in your journal. Document the context and what happened and bring the light of love and compassion to yourself and the others involved in the situation.

Engaging in this process will allow you to accept and even love your shadow self. Your shadow self is that part of yourself that you're ashamed of—you might perceive it as weak or angry or bad. It's not any of these things, however, it's just a part of yourself that has a role in your survival and coping abilities. By bringing your shadow self into the light of your self-compassion, you will give this part of you the love it needs, so you can fully accept yourself and everything that is part of you.

This is critical for your spiritual growth and awakening. If you don't fully accept and love yourself, you might have a tendency to engage in spiritual bypassing. This is where you use your spirituality as an excuse to avoid confronting unresolved emotional issues. You might think, for example, "This is just how I am and everything is perfect as it is, therefore, I don't need to do anything about it". This is a trap, because by not confronting your unresolved issues, they will continue to hinder your spiritual growth.

You might be wondering why this is particularly important. If you don't deal with your own stuff, it will make you much more vulnerable to psychic attacks from other empaths. Knowing what are truly your emotions through processing them will help you understand when you are receiving and experiencing the emotions of other people. When someone in a negative mindset projects their energies your way, you can experience a toxic reaction to these low frequency energetic emissions if you don't know how to process and identify your own energies as distinct from those of other people.

Tip #21—Fend off psychic attacks: So when you find yourself thinking repetitive negative thoughts, stop and process those emotions to determine whether or not they belong to you. If you find they are the product of a psychic attack—that is to say they are coming from someone else—practice the techniques I've discussed to both discharge that negative energy and transform it into a positive emotion. Then, you can project that positive emotion out to the world, including to the one who might be attacking you. Be sure to put up your protective shield after doing these rituals. This will help to prevent them from attacking you again.

Tip #22—Understand the different energies: Understanding the energy around you is also key to both protecting yourself and helping others to heal. It starts with understanding how energy moves through your own body. Your aura is an electromagnetic field that extends from your core to around four or five feet around your body. It's simply your energy field. Like an onion, there are layers to your aura. These layers are defined as the following and they correspond to your chakras:

- **The *Etheric* Body** – This is the first layer, which resonates at 20 cycles per minute and spreads out up to two inches beyond your physical self. This layer holds information about your physical health.

- **The *Emotional* Body** – The second layer, which extends to one to three inches from the physical body, contains your feelings.

- **The *Mental* Body** – The third layer, which extends to between three and eight inches from the body, contains your ideas, thoughts, and mental processes.

- **The *Astral* Level** – The fourth layer, which extends to about a foot from the body, represents the bridge to the spiritual realm and the astral plane.

- **The *Etheric* Template Body** – The fifth layer, which extends to about a foot and a half from the body, is thought to coexist on a different dimension. It is typically only visible to healers and clairvoyants.

- **The *Celestial* Body** – The sixth layer is where communication with the spiritual realm takes place and it is where you experience ecstasy and unconditional love. This is the layer involved in heightened levels of consciousness.

- **The *Causal* Body or Ketheric Template** – The seventh layer extends three to five feet from the body and it contains all of the other bodies. This is a reflection of everything your soul has undergone and it vibrates with God energy. This is the link to the Divine, where you accept your oneness with the universe.

Each auric layer has seven chakras and they all communicate with each other and exchange energy. That's why it's imperative to keep your energy flowing freely. These auric layers are the source of your Kundalini energy—your life force energy. As you experience a spiritual awakening, you are really experiencing a Kundalini awakening. It is the realization of the oneness of all energy and it can be very traumatic. You might experience a number of different sensations. But, never fear, there are several ways to deal with the incoming energy.

It's helpful as you connect to these different energies that you stay in tune with your psycho-energetic centers, known as chakras. There are six chakras and a seventh center, all of which can help you understand the different levels of consciousness. If one or more of them become blocked, then it will result in feelings of discomfort, disharmony, stress and even illness. These chakras all communicate with the auric chakras. The six chakras are the following:

• ***Muladhara***—The root chakra at the base of your spine; this is probably the most practical of the chakras and is more concerned with grounding and balance than purely with the realms of the spirit. This is where the lower body and the chakras meet, and it is very often considered the foundation of physical wellbeing. It helps us balance, maintain stability and generally keep things together. When it is blocked, our whole equilibrium seems to be disrupted and this can affect everything from our work to how we carry ourselves and even how we perceive ourselves physically.

• ***Svadhisthana***—the sacral chakra at the third vertebra of the sacrum; it is associated with sexual activity and also with other things like money, creativity, joy, and intimacy. When working optimally, we feel creative, self-aware, positive, and successful. People whose sacral chakras are working well seem to be bursting with energy and self-confidence. Once blocked, it is, of course, a very different story. You immediately start to feel off-balance, unmotivated, and uninspired. Without that motivation, it is difficult to lift oneself from the rut that you will have fallen into. You will not want to do much and even your sex drive will wither away.

• ***Manipura***—the navel chakra at the level of the navel on the spine; often referred to as the solar plexus. It regulates the function of the pancreas and digestive organs. When it is blocked, you will feel a loss of appetite, body shakes, palpitations increase, low self-esteem, fatigue, and anxiety.

• ***Anahata***—the heart chakra at mid-chest level; it is the point where the physical and spiritual merge and it is the foundation of our positive emotional wellbeing. It affects the health of our heart, lungs, chest, arms, and thymus gland. When it is blocked, we are susceptible to feelings of contempt, scorn, and even hate.

• ***Vishuddha***—the throat chakra, located just above the hollow of the neck; there are two signs for the empath that the throat chakra has become blocked. Either you will have trouble speaking at all, or you will speak too much and often say things that are an exaggeration or are false. In general, these will be things that make you look better in the eyes of others. The reason for this is that the lack of confidence that many empaths live with tend to make them overcompensate in one way or another. They either want to shrink away and hide from the world, or they want to portray an image of self-confidence. In a way, both of these symptoms are a way of hiding one's true self. When this chakra is blocked, you may notice physical indicators such as a sore throat, thyroid problems, or neck pain.

• ***Ajna***—the third eye chakra, located in the center of the brain and accessed through the middle of the forehead; it plays a dominant role in your intuitive abilities and clear-headed thinking. It also promotes a clear focus. When it is blocked, this leads to depression, dizzy spells, poor memory and recall, and headaches. More noticeable, perhaps, will be your sudden loss in confidence in your inner voice. Clearing the blocked third eye chakra involves sitting comfortably but upright with the eyes closed. Breathe deeply and then start to focus your mind on that point between your eyebrows. Next, imagine a purple light being focused on that point. Keep focusing on this as well as your breathing until you sense some relief.

The seventh center is not really considered a chakra, because it is the portal towards oneness. It is known as **Sahasrara** and it is referred to as the crown chakra, located at the top of your head. It promotes awareness, social consciousness, and brings feelings of serenity and deep peace of life. When it is blocked or fails to function properly, then you can experience a sense of being isolated from others, even when you are in a crowd. You might even be distressed and depressed so easily.

To connect to these energies, it is helpful to envision them as whorling vortices of bright light connecting one to the other. Allow yourself to envision that energy rising from the root chakra up through each successive center until it pours out of Sahasrara, as you connect to the universal oneness. This is your birthright. To know more details about chakras check out my book Chakra Healing for Beginners: The Complete Guide to Awaken And Balance Chakras For Self-Healing And Positive Energy

Tip #23—Dealing with positive feelings: The truth is that even positive feelings can be overwhelming. With a Kundalini awakening, you might experience bliss, grandiose feelings, and heart openings where you feel love for everyone. The key to dealing with these types of emotions is to seek grounding tools and set healthy boundaries. It's fine to enjoy the good feelings but ground yourself in the present moment and the understanding that nothing is forever. When these intense good feelings pass, you'll still be grounded and on the right path.

Tip #24—Psychic experiences: These experiences might happen from time to time, because as you awaken, the strength of your psychic connections increases and you're easily able to traverse time. You can sit with the experiences and even enjoy them, but don't become too attached to anything you experience, since these sensations, like everything, are temporary. Also, be sure to process the emotions that arise. It might also help to make use of oracle cards. These can help you to navigate the energetically charged world around you. These cards can help you and your loved ones, as well.

Tip #25—Dealing with constant insights and energetic flows: As an empath, you'll experience the energetic flows intensely and the insights will just keep coming. Write down the insights, because you're having them for a reason and they will be useful. For energetic flow, practice the techniques I've discussed to discharge negative energies and transform them into positive emotions.

Tip #26—Dealing with negative emotions: Since you'll be more open to emotional energy, you're likely to experience negative emotions, too. These could include fear, anxiety, sadness, and even terror. You could even have a panic attack. Remember to use the techniques we discussed to activate your vagus nerve and the parasympathetic nervous system. Those methods will help calm you down. Remember to stay grounded in the present moment and use the methods we talked about to process the energy.

Tip #27—Collective pain: As you open to the connectedness of all things, you might experience the collective pain of many in despair. These sensations will pass, but it is a good idea to use a meditation practice to understand what the lesson is in these sensations. Is there something you can do to help, even if it is a small contribution?

Tip #28—Vivid, lucid dreams: Lucid dreams are the kind where you physically experience the dream. You should be particularly aware of these and write them down in your journal. It's recommended that you write them down immediately upon waking. These dreams often contain messages important to your awakening experience. Reflect on the significance of any symbolism for your life and your awakened experience.

Tip #29—Physical sensations: You might experience a number of different kinds of physical sensations. These could include heat at the bottom of your spine, weight loss, weight gain, digestive issues, pressure or pain in random places, skin conditions, and autoimmune problems. It is very important to maintain a healthy diet and exercise routine in order to minimize these symptoms. It can also help to practice energy enhancing exercises, like yoga and/or get a relaxing massage.

Tip #30—Sleep disturbances: The intensity of the energy you're perceiving can certainly affect your sleep patterns. Here is where a good relaxing meditation practice will come in handy. Try the following—it has helped me on many a sleepless night:

- Lay down in a comfortable position and close your eyes;

- Focus your breath and go through 10 deep breathing inhalation/exhalation cycles;

- Become aware of your body—feel how your arms and legs feel on the bed;

- Beginning at your head, intentionally relax the muscles of your head and face, followed by your neck, then go down your body to your shoulders, arms, and chest. Notice the sensation of the muscles relaxing and the parts of your body sinking into the bed. Breathe deeply as you do this process. Now, continue down into your abdomen and legs. Let your limbs settle into a relaxed position.

- Now, turn your attention to the sounds you can hear. Separate out the sounds you hear in the background. How many do you hear? Can you hear insects in the background—crickets or cicadas? Can you hear the wind or the rain?

- Let yourself focus in on one soothing sound—perhaps the wind or the rain. Let your breathing normalize in rhythm and depth.

- Finally, let your mind drift off to sleep as you express gratitude for the quiet moments of life.

Tip #31—Dealing with overstimulation: Overstimulation is a common problem for empaths. If you are dealing with this problem, it can help to avoid large crowds, make use of noise cancellation headphones, and make time to spend in nature. This will all help deal with overstimulation.

Tip #32—Feeling overwhelmed: With all of this stimulation, it's normal to feel overwhelmed. To deal with this, you want to take a step back, focus on one thing at a time, and be gentle with yourself. Meditation and walks in nature can help to relieve feeling overwhelmed.

Tip #33—Changes in mood: You might experience sudden shifts in mood, from extreme joy and bliss to sadness or fear. Remember to sit with your feelings and process them to ensure they are indeed your emotions and not projections from someone nearby. Discharge negative energies and stay grounded in the present moment with the understanding that emotions are temporary and will pass.

Tip #34—Feeling fragmented: Because of the variety of energies you're sensing, you might feel fragmented. Using some of the meditation techniques I've discussed can help to reestablish your sense of connectedness with the universal soul.

Tip #35—Extreme sensitivity to content: You might become very sensitive to the content in various media, like the news or social media. It might be necessary to avoid these media while you practice grounding techniques to relieve your sensitivity.

The tips I've discussed here will help you to fully explore your spirituality and experience the benefits of an awakening. Remember that the richness of life is the reason we came into this form to experience. That richness includes all of the various emotions we feel, as well as the physical sensations and personal growth. We experience life and learn various coping skills and, then, if we're lucky enough to experience an empathic awakening, we remember the oneness from which we came and we can learn to help ourselves and others heal. But, we must understand how to handle the difficulties that we will still experience, even as awakened beings.

Essential Tools and Techniques Every Empath Should Know

It's important for empaths to understand the tools you have at your disposal to help soothe your overstimulated body, mind, and soul. I've spoken at length about grounding yourself and there are various tools you can use for this purpose. Let's discuss some of the methods you can easily employ:

Tip #36—Take a cold shower: This might not sound very soothing, but it stimulates your vagus nerve and activates your parasympathetic nervous system. That will help to keep you calm and grounded.

Tip #37—Massage: Massage is a great relaxation technique and massaging certain pressure points on the body stimulates the vagus nerve and, therefore, the parasympathetic nervous system. It also helps keep energy moving through the body.

Tip #38—Spend time with animals: Animals are a great way to reduce your blood pressure and calm your mind. They are always grounded in the present moment and they can help keep you grounded, too.

Tip #39—Reiki: Reiki is a form of alternative medicine that is referred to as energy healing. It became known in Japan in the late 1800s and it involves the transfer of energy from the practitioner to the patient. Like Traditional Chinese Medicine techniques, the aim of the therapy is to help reestablish the flow of the body's energy. It is believed that illness is the result of stagnated energy. The practice of reiki is believed to unblock stagnated energy, much in the same way that acupuncture or acupressure does. It can help you to reestablish a healthy flow of energy and it's a relaxing technique.

Tip #40—Music: Listening to music allows you to process your feelings in a conscious way. It deeply shifts the energy and emotions you feel and singing along stimulates the vagus nerve and, as a result, the parasympathetic nervous system.

Tip #41—Harness crystal energy: Crystals can offer you healing energy and by spending time in a crystal store, you'll feel the stones calling to you. When you feel ungrounded, use a stone to help you reestablish your sense of calm.

Tip #42—Visualizations: I've discussed the power of visualizations and they can also be used to ground you. You can use visualizations to shield yourself from unwanted energies and you can infuse yourself with the healing power of white light.

Tip #43—Affirmations: There's real scientific evidence supporting the benefits of positive affirmations (Critcher & Dunning, 2014). It's a quick way to ground yourself, especially when you're feeling overwhelmed by life. A few good affirmations include the following:

- I am one with all that is and I am one with the earth and my body.

- I am connected to Source at all times and it replenishes me constantly.

- I am like a tree—deeply rooted and grounded in the One, but flexible to the winds of life.

Remind yourself of these realities frequently. Use these affirmations or make some of your own.

Tip #44—Laughter: It's true what they say about laughter being the best medicine. A good belly laugh activates your vagus nerve and parasympathetic nervous system. So, watch a few comedians you like or a funny movie and let yourself laugh—it's good for you.

Tip #45—Chanting: Chanting, like singing, will also activate your vagus nerve and parasympathetic nervous system. A great practice is called **Kirtan Kriya**. The chant involves repetitions of the following mantra: **Sa Ta Na Ma**. Each part means the following:

- SA which is birth, the beginning, the infinity, and the totality;
- TA is life, existence, and creativity;
- NA is death, change, and transformation;
- MA is rebirth, regeneration, and resurrection.

There's even scientific evidence (Marciniak et al., 2014) that demonstrates the health benefits of chanting.

Tip #46—Smudging: Smudging is sometimes referred to as sagging. It involves burning herbs in a room or home to remove bad energy and help carry one's dreams to the universe. Smudging with sacred smoke has magical properties and benefits. It can clear away any unwanted energy in your physical space and it also clears out your mental and emotional space.

Tip #47—Essential oils: The scents of essential oils can help you feel grounded with just a few quick inhales. There are three great oils for this purpose and you should carry a scent with you everywhere you go. Just place a few drops in your palms, rub your hands together, and inhale until you once again feel grounded. The three oils that work well for this are:

- Prime Natural Anxiety Relief Blend
- DoTerra's Grounding Blend
- Young Living's Grounding Essential Oil

Tip #48—Practice Tai Chi: Grounding is at the heart of the practice of Tai Chi. The practice is about establishing a deeper connection to the ground. Practicing these ancient exercises helps you bring harmony and balance into your life.

Tip #49—Get enough sleep: The benefits of enough sleep cannot be underestimated and it's worth mentioning again. Sleep helps cleanse your mind and refresh your body. Make getting enough sleep a priority in your life.

By using these tools, you can maintain a healthy, harmonious balance in your life and you can better manage your energy. This will allow you to help yourself and others manage and control the various energies of life and it will help you overcome many of life's challenges.

The Last Tip Empaths Should Never Forget

This last tip is perhaps the most important one for the empath. It's so easy to get caught up in life, particularly since, as an empath, you are exposed to so many energetic forces. You have a gift, but to use it properly, you have to stay healthy and maintain a constant control over the energies you perceive. You have to know how to discharge negative energy and how to transform it into positive energy. You have to know how to ground yourself and how to deal with the challenges of the spiritual awakening that almost always accompanies empathic abilities. You are a spiritual being, an energetic force of nature, and your gift can help you and everyone around you to live a fuller, richer life.

I've talked about several tips for effectively managing your energy and the energetic forces that you perceive. Meditation and journaling will help you process your feelings and recognize your own emotions versus those of others around you. Chanting, singing, and deep breathing will help to activate your vagus nerve and, therefore, your parasympathetic nervous system. Smudging can help you clear your physical, mental, and emotional space and essential oils can help you ground yourself on a moment's notice. Physical exercise will help keep your physical energy high and eating right will keep you healthy and properly fuel your body. For the empath, these practices and the many more I've discussed are particularly important. But, there is one last tip that the empath should never forget.

Tip #50—Play: You came to this physical form to experience the richness of life in all its variety. You came to experience joy, sadness, triumph, failure, anger, peace, and all of the other emotional and physical sensations that life brings. So, live it, feel it, and don't forget to enjoy it. Go out and play—play like you did when you were a little kid. Children are much closer to the universal One because life hasn't gotten in their way yet. They play and imagine and do all the things that bring them joy. No matter what age you are, playing never gets old. Go out and make snow angels, skip through the park, lay on the grass, and watch the clouds go by, play fetch with your best friend, and live life to its fullest. Play, live, love, and enjoy this life you came to experience. Stay grounded in the present moment—something playing can help you do. It brings you into the joy of the moment and focuses your attention on the sensations that bring you happiness. Empaths have some of the richest lives out there because they genuinely feel all emotions so intensely. We are lucky for that and we deserve a rich life full of play!

I highly encourage you to join our friendly community Facebook to maximize the value you receive from this book. What often helps a lot is connecting with other like-minded people whom you can relate to, get support, and learn from on how to navigate Life's challenges. This can be an excellent support network for you.

It would be great to connect with you there,

To Join Our Friendly Support Group visit: http://bit.ly/2pg5AEE

Seven Powerful Crystals Every Empath Should Have

Are you feeling overwhelmed with other people's emotions?

Would you like to protect and heal your energy?

Being an empath means absorbing both the positive and negative energies

This can be both a blessing and a curse

The good news is that crystals with their unique characteristics and vibration can actually help

To balance your emotions, protect your energy and keep you grounded with these 7 powerful crystals, visit: https://bit.ly/2Y8cIkp

Finally, thank you again for grabbing my book bundle! Your opinion matters! Please share your thoughts about my book on the platform that you bought from, and don't be shy, the more information, the better.

Thank you and good luck!

Resources

Ageless Arts. (2018, February 28). Sa Ta Na Ma Meditation, a powerful tool for preventing or stopping Alzheimer's disease. Retrieved February 11, 2020, from https://agelessartsyoga.com/instructor-group-yoga/sa-ta-na-ma-meditation/

Critcher, C. R., & Dunning, D. (2014). Self-Affirmations Provide a Broader Perspective on Self-Threat. *Personality and Social Psychology Bulletin, 41*(1), 3–18. https://doi.org/10.1177/0146167214554956

Eisler, M. (2017, January 23). How to Stay Emotionally Balanced If You're an Empath. Retrieved February 4, 2020, from https://chopra.com/articles/how-to-stay-emotionally-balanced-if-you%E2%80%99re-an-empath

Ewens, H. (2018, November 8). Super Empaths Are Real, Says Study. Retrieved February 11, 2020, from https://www.vice.com/en_us/article/xwj84k/super-empaths-are-real-says-study

Familydoctor.org editorial staff. (2019, July 22). Mind/Body Connection: How Emotions Affect Health. Retrieved February 3, 2020, from https://familydoctor.org/mindbody-connection-how-your-emotions-affect-your-health/

Grace, S. (2019, January 8). How To Eat To Thrive as an Empath. Retrieved February 11, 2020, from https://www.sarahkgrace.com/blog/how-to-eat-to-thrive-as-an-empath

Greenberg, E. (2018, July 8). How to Avoid Toxic Relationships Try these five tips when you are choosing friends and mates. Retrieved February 11, 2020, from https://www.psychologytoday.com/us/blog/understanding-narcissism/201807/how-avoid-toxic-relationships

Gulla, A. (2017, November 14). 15 Things To Remember If You Love An Empath. Retrieved February 11, 2020, from https://www.lifehack.org/articles/communication/15-tips-help-you-love-empath.html

Holland, K. (2019, August 15). How to Recognize and Respond to Energy Vampires at Home, Work, and More. Retrieved February 11, 2020, from https://www.healthline.com/health/mental-health/energy-vampires#codependent

Howe, M. (2018, December 6). Energy & Empaths - National Wellness Institute. Retrieved February 11, 2020, from https://www.nationalwellness.org/blogpost/1644820/314421/Energy—Empaths

Hutchison, L. H. (2016, January 25). Exercise for Empaths: Let's Get Physical! Retrieved February 11, 2020, from https://connectingempathichelpersandartiststospirit.wordpress.com/2016/01/05/exercise-for-empaths-lets-get-physical/

Kathrine, D. (2019, August 3). Navigating Psychic Attack: A Guide for The Empath. Retrieved February 11, 2020, from https://theknowing1.wordpress.com/2013/11/13/navigating-psychic-attack/

Luna, A. (2020, January 18). How Being an Empath is Connected to Spiritually Awakening ⋆. Retrieved February 11, 2020, from https://lonerwolf.com/being-an-empath-awakening/

Magine, S. (2018, September 18). What is an Empath? Empathy, Energy and the Spectrum of Sensitivity. Retrieved February 11, 2020, from https://mechanicsofbeing.com/empath-energy-coping-spectrum-of-sensitivity/

Marciniak, R., Sheardova, K., Čermáková, P., Hudeček, D., Šumec, R., & Hort, J. (2014). Effect of Meditation on Cognitive Functions in Context of Aging and Neurodegenerative Diseases. *Frontiers in Behavioral Neuroscience*, *8*. https://doi.org/10.3389/fnbeh.2014.00017

Mystical Raven. (2019, February 6). Being An Empath Is Connected To A Powerful Spiritual Awakening. Retrieved February 11, 2020, from https://mysticalraven.com/spirituality/14548/being-an-empath-is-connected-to-a-powerful-spiritual-awakening

Nicely Done Magick. (n.d.). Empowered Empaths. Retrieved February 11, 2020, from https://www.nicelydonemagick.com/empowered-empaths.html

Orloff, J. (2014, December 2). 6 Relationship Tips for Empaths. Retrieved February 11, 2020, from https://www.elephantjournal.com/2014/12/6-relationship-tips-for-empaths/

Orloff, J. (2016, February 19). 10 Traits Empathic People Share And how to look out for yourself if you are one. Retrieved February 11, 2020, from https://www.psychologytoday.com/us/blog/emotional-freedom/201602/10-traits-empathic-people-share

Orloff, J. (2018, July 3). Are You an Introverted or Extroverted Empath? Retrieved February 11, 2020, from https://drjudithorloff.com/ask-dr-orloff/are-all-empaths-introverts/

Orloff, J. (2019, September 23). Are You an Empath? Take this 20 Question Empath Test. Retrieved February 11, 2020, from https://drjudithorloff.com/quizzes/empath-self-assessment-test/

Planetary Cymatic Resonance. (n.d.). Planetary Cymatic Resonance - BRAINWAVE STIMULATION & THERAPEUTIC SOUND Meditation. Retrieved February 4, 2020, from http://www.gravityterminal.com/event/planetary-cymatic-resonance-brainwave-stimulation-therapeutic-sound-m

Pursey, K. (2018, November 23). 6 Types of Empaths: Which One Are You and How to Make the Most of Your Gift? Retrieved February 11, 2020, from https://www.learning-mind.com/types-of-empaths/

Raghu, M. (2018). A Study to Explore the Effects of Sound Vibrations on Consciousness. *International Journal of Social Work and Human Services Practice*, *6*(3), 75–88. Retrieved from http://www.hrpub.org/download/20180730/IJRH2-19290514.pdf

Sacred Acoustics. (n.d.). Technology - Sacred Acoustics. Retrieved February 4, 2020, from https://www.sacredacoustics.com/pages/technology-app

Sage Goddess. (2019, March 28). What is Smudging and How do I Smudge? Retrieved February 11, 2020, from https://www.sagegoddess.com/how-do-i-smudge/

Soldner, J. (2017, June 18). Empaths and the Law of Attraction. Retrieved February 11, 2020, from http://www.jennifersoldner.com/2016/09/empaths-and-the-law-of-attraction.html

Stewart, E. (2016a, June 12). Empaths and Manifesting Part 1. Retrieved February 11, 2020, from https://psychicspiritart.com/2016/06/05/empaths-and-manifesting-part-1/

Stewart, E. (2016b, June 12). Empaths and Manifesting Part 2. Retrieved February 11, 2020, from https://psychicspiritart.com/2016/06/08/empaths-and-manifesting-part-2/

Tartakovsky, M. M. S. (2018, October 8). 10 Way to Build and Preserve Better Boundaries. Retrieved February 11, 2020, from https://psychcentral.com/lib/10-way-to-build-and-preserve-better-boundaries/

Team Empathy. (2018, February 13). 50 Ways To Ground Yourself As An Empath. Retrieved February 11, 2020, from https://enlightenedempathy.wordpress.com/2018/02/12/50-ways-to-ground-yourself-as-an-empath/

Tedder, L. (2018, June 8). What Energetic Connections Feel Like to an Empath. Retrieved February 11, 2020, from https://www.thespiritualeclectic.com/2014/05/06/what-energetic-connections-feel-like-to-an-empath/

The International Center for Reiki Training. (2019, September 11). What is Reiki? Retrieved February 11, 2020, from https://www.reiki.org/faqs/what-reiki

Unknown, I. (2019, July 8). Binaural Beats. Retrieved February 4, 2020, from https://www.empathguide.com/binaural-beats/

Wiest, B. (2018, October 17). 16 Signs You're Having What's Known As A Kundalini Awakening. Retrieved February 11, 2020, from https://thoughtcatalog.com/brianna-wiest/2018/08/16-signs-youre-having-whats-known-as-a-kundalini-awakening/

Don't miss out!

Visit the website below and you can sign up to receive emails whenever Alison L. Alverson publishes a new book. There's no charge and no obligation.

https://books2read.com/r/B-A-RQLJ-ORVNB

Did you love *Empath's Survival Guide: How to Develop Your gift, Set Boundaries, and Control Your Emotions (Emotional Intelligence, Empath, and Empath Workbook)*? Then you should read *Chakra Healing For Beginners: The Complete Guide to Awaken and Balance Chakras for Self-Healing and Positive Energy*[1] by Alison L. Alverson!

[2]

In a universe made of energy...

...how you control your own is essential.

Are you ready to expand your health and happiness?

To awaken, one must understand the power of the chakras. To heal one's mind, body, and spirit, one must align them. The wonders of a quiet mind allow anyone to achieve a level of joy and abundance they never knew existed.

This journey will change your life.

---

1. https://books2read.com/u/boDGZL
2. https://books2read.com/u/boDGZL

You'll learn:

- Ancient Medicine and the Use of Chakras
- Secret and Powerful Healing Techniques
- Six Mistakes Most Beginners Make in Meditation and How to Avoid Them
- How Guided Meditation Can Transform and Awaken You Spiritually
- The Mysteries and Benefits of Hindu and Buddhist Tantras
- plus, much more

Alison L. Alverson is an accomplished self-published author. She is an empath, who has spent nearly one decade, since awakening, mastering the practices. Each day will be one you can cherish once you've brought your life into alignment.

It's time to unleash the power of your chakras.

You'll love these lessons because improving your mental and physical well-being is the best thing you can do for yourself.

Get started now!

Read more at www.alisonalverson.com.

Also by Alison L. Alverson

Chakra Series Book 1
Chakra Healing For Beginners: The Complete Guide to Awaken and Balance Chakras for Self-Healing and Positive Energy

Chakra Series Book 2
Chakra Healing For Beginners: Discover 35 Self-Healing Techniques to Awaken and Balance Chakras for Health and Positive Energy

Empath Series Book 1
Empath: An Extensive Guide for Developing Your Gift of Intuition to Thrive in Life

Empath Series Book 2
Empath Workbook: Discover 50 Successful Tips To Boost your Emotional, Physical And Spiritual Energy

Standalone

Emotional Intelligence : 21 Effective Tips To Boost Your EQ (A Practical Guide To Mastering Emotions, Improving Social Skills & Fulfilling Relationships For A Happy And Successful Life)
Empath's Survival Guide: How to Develop Your gift, Set Boundaries, and Control Your Emotions (Emotional Intelligence, Empath, and Empath Workbook)

Watch for more at www.alisonalverson.com.

About the Author

Alison L. Alverson is an American and accomplished self-published author. She is an empath, who has spent nearly one decade, since awakening, mastering her empathic nature. She studied various psychological techniques and attended spiritual healing workshops from a variety of traditions.

She has a burning passion and an open spirit to help empaths, who are the healers, the nurturers, and the highly sensitive persons, manage their empathy without getting drained and teach them strategies to thrive as an empath by sharing with them her experiences and practical tips that helped her. She wants to grow continuously, and she wants to encourage empaths to do the same through taking consistent actions.

Alison loves to travel and finds her passion in writing books. She is a social person and loves sitting with people and listening to them. In her free time, she likes taking photos, especially outdoors, and listening to the sound of nature. Alison loves to hear from her dear readers.

Feel free to email her at alisonalverson12@gmail.com

Read more at www.alisonalverson.com.

www.ingramcontent.com/pod-product-compliance
Ingram Content Group UK Ltd.
Pitfield, Milton Keynes, MK11 3LW, UK
UKHW020123290926
15471UKWH00003B/247

9 798201 529482